A CHRISTMAS

TO REMEMBER

A CHRISTMAS

TO REMEMBER

A COLLECTION OF FAVORITE HOLIDAY MEMORIES

Deseret Book Company
Salt Lake City, Utah

Library of Congress Cataloging-in-Publication Data

A Christmas to remember.
    p. cm.
  ISBN 0-87579-410-6
  1. Christmas. I. Deseret Book Company.
GT4985.C544
394.2′6828—dc20   90-39263
                                                CIP

Printed in the United States of America

10   9   8   7   6   5   4   3   2   1

CONTENTS

CHRISTMAS IN AFRICA

Mary Ellen Edmunds

The Christmas of 1984 began in September when I arrived in Nigeria, West Africa, with Ann Laemmlen to help establish a health project for children and families. The feeling and spirit of Christmas were there from the beginning of the adventure, perhaps because we were experiencing something new and unusual. Further, our awareness was heightened as our chances to learn important lessons expanded. The season was not a "White Christmas" kind, but one of beautiful black faces, green trees, flowers, mud homes, "termite castles," drums, rain, and so much more.

We left Lagos for Eket, Cross River State, on Friday, September 14, 1984, and drove for ten hours through the rain forest area of Nigeria. The scenery was spectacular. There we were in the midst of a *National Geographic* article! We were fascinated by the little trails leading off into the bush from the expressway, wondering who lived down those trails and what life was like for them. We had a feeling of wanting to know all those people, young and old, whose faces were filled with life—with sorrow, serenity, curiosity, suffering, wisdom.

Christmas that year was life in The Palace. When we arrived we gave our home that name, probably with some snickering about how much of a palace it *wasn't.* It was big and empty—no shelves, chairs, beds, tables, stools. It was the color of cement plus blue, pink, lavendar, and yellow. Gracious living, you bet! Lizards everywhere, all sizes and colors. There was a jungle-like area on the east side of our palace that we promptly named "The Enchanted Forest," where, we were promised, lived many deadly snakes. And to the back of the home were fields, like a quilt, with small, many-shaped patches of cassava belonging to different families, all connected but carefully measured.

We began fixing up The Palace: a few lines of rope on which to hang clothes; iron bars on doors and windows so that mosquitoes and cockroaches weighing more than two hundred pounds couldn't come in; beds made by our neighbor Sunday, the carpenter; shelves and tables made with the help of our branch president, Samuel, and our wonderful missionary neighbors; plants brought in to make it beautiful (which amazed our neighbors, who hadn't thought of bringing any plants or flowers *inside* because they're in such abundance *outside*); a tall plastic garbage can with a toilet plunger to be our washer (for clothes).

Gradually our home became The Palace. We watched as children came to visit. They were fascinated with the floors, and loved bringing small rocks to play with on the smooth surface, and walking around with their bare feet experiencing a brand-new sensation. They looked at the taps (which occasionally had water dropping out of them) as if they were magic.

Our chapel was a mud room about fifteen feet square. We had to duck to go in the doorway without hitting our heads. At our first meeting the room felt like an oven to us. People crowded against each other. There were a variety of chairs and two tables. Streamers hung from the ceiling, just like at a service station. A few signs and posters adorned the walls, most with the appearance of having been used previously in another church. A copy of the Articles of Faith in Efik, the local language, was available.

There were many, many children, all of them curious, but not shy for long. All the women and girls had their heads covered. Thirty-three attended, and we kept wondering how all those bodies got inside that small room. They sang with *great* enthusiasm—we

thought they'd literally raise the roof. Even the little children seemed to know all the words of all the hymns and sang with joy. There was no organ or piano, so whoever was leading would hum the first few notes of the hymn (usually with the congregation humming along), then count "one, two, go!" and we'd begin. The volume was almost enough to hurt our ears. The favorite hymn seemed to be "God Moves in a Mysterious Way." When the sacrament was passed we got a shock: the water tasted like fire water. It burned all the way down! We found out they had boiled the water in a pot in which they had cooked hot pepper soup.

We were taught about "neat and tidy homes" in Relief Society. Our teacher was named Comfort, and she taught so carefully. At one point she held up her manual with a picture of a "neat and tidy home." Having never seen one quite like it, she inadvertently held it upside down. Everyone looked intently. And it struck me that they were filled with a desire to live the gospel of Jesus Christ with all their hearts and with total obedience. There were so many words and phrases in the lesson that they could not understand but hoped to apply: "thrift stores," "auctions," "quilting," "bring luster to the dull." These were great Latter-day Saints who put clean mud on all their walls, inside and out, each four to six months. In the lesson mothers were encouraged to help their children clean a drawer. The African sisters wondered, "What is a drawer?"

One prelude to Christmas that year was a youth conference in a nearby branch, which lasted for many hours and included a six-act, fifty-four-scene drama about Esau and Jacob. The scenes lasted anywhere from thirty seconds to three minutes. We were amazed that the thin green curtain, on a string that kept knotting, was opened and closed over one hundred times with so few problems. Only once did it fall completely down. That part of the program closed with six girls singing "The Six Letters of Christ," a song they had no doubt learned in another church.

Christmas in Nigeria is an adventure in gratitude—gratitude for a breakfast of bread with banana, or for a "spit bath" with three cups of water while listening for the water to drip from the tap so we could run and save every drop. (We always put "bathe" in quotes in our journal.) Gratitude is harvesting the rain in the middle of the night in every available container and singing along with Albert Fallows on a tape "The Spirit of God." It's a gift from the chief who lives near us of a huge stock of bananas too heavy for one person to carry (transformed in the days that followed into *much* banana bread). It's wishing you could put a nativity scene among the pineapple in the front yard and flock all the trees in "The Enchanted Forest."

Christmastime in West Africa is bites from mosquitoes, fleas, bedbugs, and the ever-clever "No See'ums." It's a perfect place to test Off! against Skin-

so-Soft. It's termites in our wooden spoons. These are the same termites that created a family-tree mural on one wall. It's Harmattan—the time of year when the Sahara Desert blows south and you can see the dust in the air. It's finding out that a baby in Calabar has been named Calvin Crane and one in Eket is Sylvester. It's fireflies in our bedroom and watching the candle drip on the many nights when there was no electricity. (We made a magnificent wax museum, with bugs and beasts in lifelike poses. No one seemed to want to come to see it, however.) It's hooking up our neighbor missionary, Elder Madsen, with a sprayer full of Ambush 25 and having him douse the whole area. It's neighbors fixing soup with seventy-five snails in it. We found we were gathering so many wonderful recipes. . . .

Christmas of 1984 was the gift of answers to prayers for safety and protection. One day we were driving from the city of Calabar back to our home in Eket with a trunk full of Church materials. We were stopped at a checkpoint, and the guards with guns demanded that we "open the boot!" I did so. And there it was—all the pamphlets and materials. Another officer said in a rather rough voice, "What are all these things?" I replied, "These are Church materials, Sir." Quickly he said, "Shut it—we love God!" And off we went, grateful for the blessing. We stopped a few minutes later and bought three "Christmas trees." We found some Ironwood branches and gave one to each of our two neighbor couples and kept one for The Palace. We "flocked" our branch with tiny pieces of cotton colored with felt pens, and we attached a star that the "tree" couldn't support, so we pasted it on the wall. On Christmas Day we had enough water for a shower and washing our hair. It was a Christmas of simple gifts and deep gratitude.

Christmas is children—the little children of Africa, carrying heavy loads of water from the river to their homes, laughing and responding to us and each other. We loved watching them mimicking us, especially when they didn't know we were watching. It's one small child we nicknamed "Grizzly" who must have been afraid of Ann because she always attacked when she came near. It's wide-eyed children looking with wonder on a little battery-operated electronic organ for the first time, and offering tiny fingers to push a key and bring music into the neighborhood. It's small children who are ill and feel pain and hunger, whose faces show no hope and who soak up all the love you can give them. We found ourselves wanting to do so much more than we had time or health or strength or other resources for. Our hearts ached for the hunger, the suffering, the discouragement and all that we saw. Tears were always very, very close. We yearned to do good things that would help the little children. It would have been so hard to know about all of that without being in a position to do anything.

Our gifts to others that Christmas included sharing the gospel of Jesus Christ, helping weigh and measure the children, helping people make water filters and learn to purify their water, sharing information about budgeting and nutrition. Most of the gifts we gave could not be wrapped. A few days before Christmas the missionaries took the portable generator to the place we now rented as a chapel so we could show "The First Vision" filmstrip to members and friends. The generator made so much noise that no one could hear the words or music, but it didn't matter. It was as thrilling as anything that had ever happened in that neighborhood. I was sitting near Brother EtukAkpan, who had recently been baptized, and when Joseph Smith's vision was portrayed Brother EtukAkpan was so moved that he jumped up and clapped and shouted, "Hallelujah! Hallelujah!"

At this branch Christmas program, I reached out my arms to little Blessing, a neighbor child. She hesitated a long while but eventually held out her tiny arms for me to pick her up. I hugged her tightly, then held her and looked into her eyes. She looked up at me and, in an unusual response, did not look away for a long time. She was hot with a fever, and her skin was very dry. She had sores on her head and feet. Her stomach was puffy. Once I put my hand on her lap with the palm up, and by and by a tiny black hand was put in my hand, and I cried. I sat with tears running down my face as I thought about little Blessing and what her life was like, and how different her experiences were from those of my childhood. "Oh, Blessing," I thought, "you need enough to eat, a birthday party, a new dress, a smile. . . ."

The highlight of the Christmas of 1984 began on the evening of Saturday, December 8, when we went to a beautiful village called Assong with our neighbor missionaries. Assong was off the main road and onto a narrow path through the beautiful jungle. What a pleasant time of evening, with everyone either home or on their way, walking, visiting. Children were laughing and playing, especially wherever there was a stream of water. Naked children were everywhere—jumping, splashing, bathing, squealing, filling containers to carry home. Out in the villages there was a sweet feeling of unity, friendliness and neighborliness.

We arrived at a large building where a congregation had requested lessons about The Church of Jesus Christ of Latter-day Saints. We sat on wooden benches with one kerosene lantern for light and listened as Elder Tretheway taught a discussion that was translated for the audience by a local Church member.

I was sitting next to someone who was quietly answering each question before it was translated into Efik. Finally I turned to see who this person was. "You know the answers to these questions." "Yes, Ma'am." "How do you know the answers?" "I am studying, Ma'am." "What is your name?"

"My name is Sylvester, Ma'am." "How old are you, Sylvester?" "I am twelve years old, Ma'am." "Sylvester, do you believe what you are learning?" "Yes, Ma'am, and I will be baptized, and then I will be a dee-ah-con." I came to love this boy who was so responsive to the gospel of Jesus Christ.

A few days later we went back to Assong with Elder and Sister Tretheway to help the people hold a sacrament meeting. For the first time they sang "I Need Thee Every Hour," "We Thank Thee, O God, for a Prophet" (having so recently learned there *was* a prophet), "How Great the Wisdom and the Love," "I Am a Child of God," and "Silent Night." Close to one hundred attended. They were so reverent and respectful. It was one of the sweetest sacrament meetings of my life. We had some "competition" further up the road. A congregation was having a religious meeting, and it sounded like a program at the Polynesian Cultural Center, with drums and clapping and bells and people dancing. We had a musical number: a group of youth sang "It's Not an Easy Road We're Traveling to Heaven." When the meeting finished, no one left. They seemed to want to keep the feeling with them. Within a few days, fifty-eight people were ready to be baptized.

One of the best gifts that year was the gift Elder Tretheway gave to the people in Assong and their friends from other villages. He worked hard to assure that all the ordinances performed on Friday, December 28, were carried out by local African priesthood holders. We met in the building in Assong on that day. When we arrived, all the future members were there waiting. Some were asleep, stretched out on the wooden benches; they had apparently been waiting a long time. And indeed, they and so many others in Africa *have* waited a long time for the gospel, the priesthood, the ordinances, the knowledge that their Redeemer lives.

One of the first persons I saw was Sylvester Akpan Essien, my friend and brother. I had for him a letter and a bar of soap from a young Boy Scout in Mapleton, Utah, who was in my mother's troop back home. Sylvester was thrilled! I loved watching his face. He looked like an angel. I said to him, "Sylvester, you are my *brother*." He smiled and said, "I know." Then I said, "I love you, Sylvester." He said, "I know." A week later he was ordained a deacon.

It was a tremendous thrill when from the back of the room the Melchizedek Priesthood holders of that part of Africa came forward, in their white shirts, with all the dignity and majesty of sons of God. I was deeply moved in that moment as Daniel, Samuel, Donatus, Frank, Malachai, and David walked to the front of the room and sat on the stand. There was such serenity and peace! The lump in my throat was enormous. We sang "I Know That My Redeemer Lives." There was a feeling of reverence and readiness on the part of the whole congregation. This was a day they had waited for much longer than we or they realized. Donatus spoke

about baptism. And then the large group was divided into three smaller groups of about twenty each. There was a leader appointed to each group, a helper, a "baptizer," and a recorder (I was pleased to be assigned as recorder to Sylvester's group).

And we began the trek to the river. I shall never forget the joy of watching those great souls walk quickly and reverently toward the river. Villagers came to the edge of the trail to say hello and wish them well; they seemed to be aware that something special was happening.

The site for the baptism was made to order. Some people who were bathing were kindly asked if they could let us use the place for a while, which they did. *Lots* of people gathered to watch, even though they didn't fully understand what was happening. And then the people went into the bushes to change into white, and it began to look even more beautiful and holy in that sacred, peaceful place. Each of the three groups chose a separate location, close to each other but far enough away so that there would be no distraction from one group to another.

And then it began. The baptism of fifty-eight wonderful children of God, one by one. This surely is one of the most tender, spiritual, unforgettable experiences of my life. I loved watching the faces of those who came up out of the water with such joy and happiness. I felt tender towards the older woman who, at the time she was interviewed, realized by the look on the faces of the missionary and interpreter that she wasn't answering correctly. She eventually said that she knew she couldn't remember details, but she *knew* that she had finally found the Savior and his Church, and *please* could she be baptized.

I was touched that those who were baptized first quickly changed so that others could use the white clothing; there wasn't enough for one per person. There was patience and love evident in every act. An older man with twisted feet had to use a cane, and was helped tenderly into the river and later back to the shore.

With prior permission, several of the men were brought to the shore of the river and confirmed members of the Church, then ordained priests and allowed to go back in the river and baptize their families. As long as I have a memory I will see a picture of Elder Tretheway kneeling in the mud on the shore, slowly helping a man baptize his wife, word by word, until he got it right. When he finally was through, everyone clapped for joy.

When all had been baptized, we walked back to the building, which had now become a chapel. We watched with awe as they walked in, smiling at us and at each other. Our branch president, Samuel, talked about the Holy Ghost, and then all who had not yet been confirmed were confirmed. Our district president, Daniel Tom Usen, welcomed these new members of the Church. We then sang "God Be with You," and everyone waved during the chorus.

I watched Elder Tretheway during these moments, knowing how hard he had worked to "do as little as possible" and let this be a day when neighbor helped and served neighbor. He said to me, "This is the greatest day of my life!" I know he helped make it so for many others as well.

We drove back to Eket accompanied by a magnificent sunset reflected in the Qua Ibo River. Merry, Merry Christmas! Christmas is love, and I shall always remember the love that was shared by so many wonderful friends in a small village in Africa in 1984. Peace on earth, good will towards men, everywhere.

A KISSY KISSY CHRISTMAS

Louise Plummer

It was the Christmas when I liked Ike. He had just won his second presidential election, and he and Mamie grinned at us from the cover of *Life* magazine. It was a Christmas of Perry Como and Bing Crosby specials; and the regulars, Russell Arms and Snookie Lanson and all the *Hit Parade* singers and dancers, still entertained us on Saturday nights. We hardly ever listened to the radio anymore. That Christmas I played my hi-fi, but instead of Christmas carols, I played "Your Kisses Take Me to Shangrila" by the Four Coins until the record grooves wore out. That Christmas I was fourteen, and I wanted to be kissed more than I wanted to breathe.

Don't get me wrong. I didn't want to be kissed by just anyone. I wanted to be kissed by *him. One and Only.* I hadn't met him, but I knew that when I did, our "eyes would lock forever," an expression I found in the *Ladies' Home Journal.* I didn't want him simply to kiss and run, or worse, kiss and tell. I wanted him to declare his love, marry me, and carry me away to the Forbushes' basement apartment, conven-

iently located across the back alley behind my parents' house. I would then exchange recipes with my mother and save crossword puzzles for my father. Mother and Dad would see that he was making me blissfully happy, and so there would be no need for them to worry about their fourteen-year-old married daughter.

That Christmas I spent part of my allowance on a sprig of mistletoe wrapped in cellophane with a meager red ribbon tied to the stem. I hung it on my bedroom wall above the half-dozen pictures of Tab Hunter carefully pasted above my bed. Tab Hunter with a redhead. Tab Hunter with a blonde. Tab Hunter with a brunette. The caption insisted he liked all types of girls as long as they had a nice sense of humor (which was about all I had to recommend me at age fourteen). Tab Hunter with horses. Tab Hunter on Malibu Beach and Tab Hunter with his mother. Tab Hunter never kissed a girl on the first date. I respected Tab Hunter. He would have been my first choice for kissing, marrying, and settling down in the Forbushes' apartment. But I knew

8

reality from fantasy. He was just a picture on the wall. I needed someone real with real lips.

The real lips turned out to belong to Derek Scofield, whose parents owned the rest home on Ninth East. He was three years older than I, and he *belonged* to my friend and next-door neighbor, Myrna Kitchner. Actually, he was her interim boyfriend. She had gone all of her life with Leroy Bench, whom she eventually married; but that Christmas there had been a serious schism of sorts, and now Derek Scofield, who had a murky resemblance to Rock Hudson, was her boyfriend. Myrna revealed to me in hushed secrecy that he was a good kisser. The concept that kissing could be evaluated as good or bad was new to me; nevertheless, I was impressed. Because of Derek Scofield, Myrna was the only one of my friends who sat in the Emigration Ward show with a boy.

One doesn't hear much about ward shows anymore, but in those days the Friday night ward show was a significant part of my social life. I never missed them and neither did my friends. My father, who was the elders' quorum president, was responsible for choosing the films and running the projector. He had ordered for that particular Christmas season *Miracle on 34th Street* from the film catalog that we luckily got to keep at our house. But what arrived were two reels of *Miracle* and a third reel of some other movie, a cowboy movie, that had absolutely nothing to do with Christmas or miracles. Frustrated, my father called the distributors who were apologetic but unable to set things right; so instead of *Miracle on 34th Street,* we received a movie that had nothing to do with Christmas but which starred Fernando Lamas and Esther Williams.

For me, at fourteen, this was better than *Miracle on 34th Street.* For one thing, Esther Williams was one of my favorite movie stars, and for another, I knew that she and Fernando Lamas would be kissing a lot. And, theoretically, I liked kissing. Besides, I'd already seen *Miracle on 34th Street* a dozen times.

So it was with a whole lot of anticipation that I stepped out of my front door that Friday night to attend the ward show. The first thing I saw was a light snow falling, a sign that life really did follow romantic song lyrics, because I *had* been dreaming of a white Christmas; now it seemed a real possibility. The second thing I saw was Myrna standing on her porch with Derek. I could tell by their bent postures that she was sulking and he was placating her.

"What did I do?" he asked.

She leaned against the screen door, silent.

"Hi," I called over. "Are you guys going to the ward show?"

They stared at me as if I were a talking tree. Then, at the same time, he said "yes" and she said "no."

"I don't want to go," she said, heaving an enormous sigh. "I don't feel good."

"Come on," he begged.

"No. Why don't you go with Louise?"

His head turned and considered me briefly. Like Belshazzar, I must have been weighed in the balance and found wanting, for he turned back to Myrna and begged again. "Pleeeze," he begged.

She shook her head.

Then, to my surprise, Derek Scofield said that he thought he would go with me and walked down the porch steps. When he reached the sidewalk, he swiveled around to see if Myrna was going to call him back, but she was already inside the screen door. He waited until she disappeared into the house, until the front porch light blinked off. Then he shrugged his shoulders, buried his hands deep into the pockets of his car coat and, almost passing me on the sidewalk, said, "Let's go."

I had never had any trouble talking to Derek Scofield when he was Myrna's date, but now that he was *my* date, even though it was by default, I grew tongue-tied. It wasn't that I had never dated before. I had been to two Junior Gold and Green Balls weighed down by corsages larger than my chest, but I hadn't been able to speak on those occasions either. In my mind, dating was equated with romance, not friendship. I was pretty comfortable with friendships even with boys, but I needed a scriptwriter for romance.

We walked side by side in the snow, which was now sticking to the sidewalk. From my peripheral vision, I was pleased to see that Derek was several inches taller than I was and that he had a remarkable resemblance to Rock Hudson. They could have been brothers. He smelled of Aqua Velva aftershave. We walked up the driveway, wordlessly, entered the church through the back door, and went up the stairs into the foyer, where the Christmas tree stood with large colored lights, red balls, and silver icicles meticulously hung by Sister Wannamaker, the custodian's wife.

As we entered the recreation hall, I searched for my friends, Joyce Archer and Mary Ellen Schricker, and was disappointed when I couldn't see them. What was the point of having a date at the ward show if none of your friends was there to see the event? My dad was stringing film through the projector, and I walked over to him. Here was a man I could talk to. "Are we going to have a cartoon?" I asked. Dad looked up briefly and nodded. "Hi Derek," he said. "Better sit down; we're ready to roll."

I followed Derek to the third row from the front. "Is this okay?" he asked. He actually spoke to me. I didn't like to sit up that far but would rather have had polio than object. Derek hung his arm casually on the back of my folding chair, and I wiped my sweaty palms onto my peddle pushers. The cartoon was about Mickey Mouse trying to decorate a Christmas tree, with Pluto getting in the way and ruining it all the time.

I glanced sideways at Derek and saw his Adam's apple move up and down.

He turned to me and offered me some Sen Sens. I didn't know if this was a hint about my breath or if it was an offer of refreshment. I put the Sen Sens in my mouth. They left an aftertaste of soap.

The feature film began. I loved Esther Williams and wished I could relax and enjoy the movie. It wasn't long before Esther, adorned with rubber flowers, was swimming underwater. I marvelled at the way she could smile without choking. She and Fernando Lamas were attracted to each other from the beginning of the movie. Their eyes were always locking. They were going to kiss soon. I could tell by the swelling violins in the background. Kissing scenes were usually my favorite, but now with Derek Scofield sitting next to me, I began to be embarrassed. I wished they wouldn't, but they did, and when they did, Derek Scofield reached over and kissed me. On the mouth. I was too surprised to remember to close my eyes. I saw his two eyes become one. I saw individual hairs of his eyebrows and the pores of his skin. I smelled Aqua Velva and Sen Sens. But I felt nothing. Derek Scofield did not take me to Shangrila.

I immediately became a philosopher. Why had he kissed me? I asked myself. He hardly knew me. I wasn't his girlfriend; Myrna was. Shouldn't we talk first and then kiss? I desperately wished he would lean over and say something funny, something hilarious. I wanted to laugh. I, silly girl, wanted a reason for his kissing me.

The violins were building up to another kissing scene. Apparently, the first kiss had merely whetted Fernando Lamas's Latin appetite. This time he Crushed Esther Williams to Him Passionately. He "ate her alive," as Joyce Archer was fond of saying. Derek Scofield lurched from his chair and grabbed me so awkwardly and violently that I thought my folding chair was in danger of collapsing. His kiss was wet and slightly off-center. He had both arms clasped tightly around me, and the only thing that prevented our being one flesh, as it said in the Bible — at least I thought that's what it said in the Bible — was my handbag, which I clutched against my chest like a shield. His buttons pressed into my arm. I held my breath until it was over. My neck was sore when I leaned back in my chair.

I decided some things. I decided Derek Scofield's hormones were triggered by what he saw, and what he saw was Fernando Lamas and Esther Williams kissing. When they did, he did. I decided he would have kissed Eleanor Roosevelt just as violently if she had been sitting next to him. That being the case, I decided that Derek Scofield had kissed me for the last time.

Having seen a hundred similar movies, I knew there would be more kissing scenes than I could deal with. How could I tell him that I didn't want to be kissed anymore? I couldn't. I'd rather tell him I had to go to the bathroom, and I'd never do that.

Instead, I sat forward in my seat,

both feet squarely planted on the floor, both elbows on my knees, and both hands clamped against my Sweetheart Pink mouth as if I had hoof-and-mouth disease. It was difficult watching the movie in that position. In fact, it was difficult breathing. My handbag guarded my chest.

Esther Williams and Fernando Lamas had the inevitable disagreement and then the inevitable making-up period, accompanied by much passionate kissing. I was glad I was prepared.

Derek Scofield leaned forward and asked, "What's the matter?"

"Nothing," I mumbled from behind my hands.

"Why have you got your hands on your mouth?" Suddenly he wanted to communicate. "Are you sick?"

I shook my head. He wouldn't see my mouth again while I lived.

He slumped back in his seat.

When the movie was over we walked home as we had come, without speaking. The kissing and marriage fantasies of that Christmas season washed over me like waves of nausea. Tab Hunter made me sick. The Four Coins made me sick. Esther Williams and Fernando Lamas made me sick. Mostly I, Louise Roos, with my delusions of romantic grandeur, made myself sick. I wanted to throw up.

By the time Christmas rolled around about a week-and-a-half later, I had already thrown the pictures of Tab Hunter away as well as the mistletoe. I threw away "Your Kisses Take Me to Shangrila." I didn't kiss again until I was twenty years old and dating the man who would be my husband. He talked to me (and I talked back), and he made me laugh, and laughter, as it turns out, is the best aphrodisiac of all.

A FATHER'S CHRISTMAS ANSWER

S. Michael Wilcox

I have tried to write this story many times. Each time I've failed, but the memory of my father carrying my infant son on his shoulders at Temple Square last Christmas keeps turning in my mind. I see all the tiny lights adorning the trees, like stars in a miniature universe. It is very cold and the frost sharpens the light's rays like a razor. My son is content sitting so high on his grandfather's shoulders. My mind returns to a sacred moment of my childhood—the first memory of my life. My father is holding me on his shoulders. In the background there is a turning ferris wheel covered with colored lights. My hands are on his cheeks, and I am happy. To this day I can still feel the stubble of his beard against my palms. There is a faint smell of distant trees and a sound of music.

There were not many memories that followed. A few months after my first birthday, my father left and did not return. As I grew older I came to understand the meaning of the words *divorce* and *temple annulment*. From that time on, all my memories centered on my mother.

There were moments during my childhood when I wondered why my father had left. I was never told the reasons. When we spoke of my father, the conversation centered on the role he played in my mother's conversion and deep testimony, a testimony that came as he read to her the Book of Mormon day after day.

As a young man I attended Brigham Young University. I did not intend to grow close to my father when I came to Utah, but I felt Elijah's spirit within, driving me to find my ancestral fathers. Their records were in Salt Lake City, where my father resided. He smoked and he drank during my first visit to his home. Almost everything about his life-style was foreign to me. It was hard to picture him reading the Book of Mormon. But as I visited with him, I could not deny the feeling in my heart, and I came to love him deeply. Malachi's promise was true in a very unexpected way. My heart turned to my father.

Sometime during that year a resolve began to grow inside me. I would bring my father back. I would lead him to love the Lord and his gospel. We had many conversations during my weekend visits. In one of those conversations my father explained to me that he did not believe that he had ever had an answer to prayer. To his knowledge, God had not once spoken to him. I felt this was a key to his return.

One day I felt impressed to write a book about my life. I did not begin with any illusions that it would ever be published. I simply felt a need to put down on paper my experiences as a child and as a young man. I did not intend it to deal with my father or my life without him, but as I began to write, I discovered his loss was a major focus of my life. When I knew it would be published, I put it in a box, mailed it to my father, and waited. Ten days passed, and then one night, about two in the morning, the phone rang, and I heard my father's voice. He was crying. His voice was low, almost a whisper that faded into long silences. Over and over again he said, "I'm sorry, I didn't know. I just didn't know. I never believed that I was ever missed. I never believed I ever counted or that my absence was a sorrow or concern for anyone. Will you forgive me?"

I didn't do much talking, but listened and waited through the long silences. For the first time in my life I heard him say the words whose fulfillment would become one of the most satisfying experiences of my life. "I want to be a father now. I want to be a grandfather to my grandchildren. Will you help me come back?"

The next year was very difficult for my father. He had chosen to walk a hard road. He took the temple recommend questions and one by one tried to put his life in order. Old friendships had to be broken, which left him alone. He went back to church. He gave up drinking and began paying tithing and fast offerings. And with the help of a wonderful bishop and quorum leaders, he made the transition from inactive to active. He felt a need to make amends with my sisters with whom he had not been very close over the years. He began to read the scriptures, *The Miracle of Forgiveness,* and other Church publications.

There were two hurdles that were very difficult for him. He felt a need to confess the mistakes he had made to his bishop. He called me the night before he was to go in. He was terrified. Would the bishop understand? What would he do? There were over thirty years of life to talk about. We fasted for him and somehow he found the courage. His bishop was gentle, loving, and forgiving, and this hurdle was overcome.

The last hurdle was the greatest. My father smoked. It was the only thing that stood in his way of receiving a temple recommend. For months he tried to quit. He used every method he could think of, but he could not go much longer than a few days. I tried to encourage him as best I could, but I knew as the months passed that he was losing faith in himself.

My children knew that their grandfather smoked because he would take

14

walks down the street when he visited, and his clothes always smelled of tobacco. My eldest daughter was eight at the time and had seen a film in elementary school on smoking. She came home very disturbed one afternoon and told us she was sad because her grandfather was going to die. I asked her what she meant. She told me of the film and the pictures of black lungs and said she knew her grandfather smoked and she didn't want him to die. We spoke for a few moments, but I knew that I had not said anything to her that was reassuring.

My eldest daughter has always had a deep love and faith in God. When she was little it was always such a delight to listen to her prayers. She came down from her room the next morning and said, "I talked to Heavenly Father about Grandpa, Daddy. He told me that if I asked Grandpa to quit smoking, he would." There was something in her voice, a conviction, that told me it was true. It was all so simple to her. She would ask him, and he would quit so he wouldn't die. She had talked to her Heavenly Father. Perhaps all that was needed was the faith of a child. I told her she could speak with her grandpa when he came in a few weeks to visit. This was in the fall of 1983.

When my father came I watched my daughter struggle with her emotions. She was very nervous, and I knew she was frightened. She waited till the last day of his visit, and then one afternoon, while he was sitting in the chair in the living room, she walked alone in

to talk with him. I sensed this was the moment and stood by the kitchen door, out of sight, and listened.

"Grandpa," she said, "I love you, and I don't want you to die."

My father smiled, put his arm around her, and said, "Why Kirsten, I'm not going to die."

"Yes you are," she answered, "because you smoke."

There was a long pause. My father started crying, and then Kirsten said, "But I prayed for you, Grandpa, and Heavenly Father told me that if I asked you to quit, you would quit. So I'm asking." There was a long silence while we all waited. Then my father said, "The next time you see me, Kirsten, I will have quit. I promise you." I did not tell my father I had heard the conversation. We said our good-byes later that day, and he went home. I waited for weeks for the phone call that would announce his victory over tobacco, but it never came.

This brings me to December 1983. That Christmas both my father and I received wonderful gifts from God. Both were unexpected.

I had been troubled by nightmares about my children and my wife. One summer I had taken my wife swimming in the ocean off the coast of southern California, where I grew up. A riptide caught us and pulled us out beyond the breakers. I was a good swimmer and could get back in, but my wife could not fight the tide. We both thought we would drown. I felt nearly helpless as I tried to push my wife back to the beach against the tide, feeling the waves pulling us out with every effort. I finally succeeded, but it had left awful memories.

In my dreams I was in the water with my family. They were struggling and I could not save them. No matter how hard I fought the waves, with each new curl they were further away. They kept calling for me to help them, but the waves took them out to sea. I was the only one who made it back to the beach. The nightmares were horrible, and I would wake up shaking. For days I carried with me the forlorn feeling of having lost my family.

Just before Christmas I learned the meaning of my dreams and received my gift. I was asked to speak at a fireside on families. I had decided to speak about the influence of my mother, how patient she was with me, and the nature of her love. I was finishing my talk when my oldest son walked into the room with his little brother. It was a life-changing moment that I fear I will not be able to explain.

The room grew very quiet, and I felt my Father in Heaven enter and stand behind my boys. He brought to my mind all of the wonderful memories of the moments I had spent with my sons. We had carved pumpkins together on Halloween. They had blown out the candles on their birthday cakes and with eagerness opened their presents. I thought of Christmas mornings and the light in their eyes as they asked me if Santa Claus had come. I thought of walks by the pond watching the turtles

dive and catching lizards, snakes, and polliwogs. I thought of Easter morning, hunting for eggs the Easter bunny had hid. I remembered the time I watched my son Ben pull his first trout out of the same fishing hole where I had caught my first trout over twenty-five years before. I thought of kneeling by my sons' beds, listening to them pray, and of their first talks in Sunday School. The memories flooded over me. All the happy, joyful things, the innocent insignificant incidents of childhood that I shared with my sons, flowed through me. And then the Lord asked a single question, "Would you be the son raised without a father or the father who lost his son?" My sons left the room and I cried, long and hard and uncontrollably, for hours for my father.

I understood for the first time in my life all he missed. The fathers'-and-sons' outings, my baptism and confirmation, the priesthood ordinances, the Little League—the thousand and one tiny moments of a boy's life were not a part of my father's memory. What a fullness of irrecoverable joy he gave up! God let me walk in his shoes, and I knew then the meaning of my dreams and the forlorn, desperate feeling of watching my wife and children being carried out by the waves. I knew the peace of total forgiveness, and how easy forgiveness comes when we truly understand one another. I did not speak about my mother that night; I spoke of fatherhood and the great privilege God grants to ordinary men to be fathers who share memories with children.

I have never received in all my life a greater Christmas gift than that. But unknown to me at that time, my father was receiving his own gift that Christmas. He had failed in all his efforts to quit smoking. After talking to my daughter, he had tried every week. On Monday he would quit, but by the end of the week the need was so great that he would smoke again.

The week before Christmas he had promised himself that he would give his family a Christmas gift. He would conquer tobacco by Christmas. He tried all that week, but on Christmas morning the need was too great and he smoked again. Broken in spirit and full of despair, he went to see his brother for Christmas dinner. The first thing my uncle asked him when he came in the door concerned his smoking habit. "Have you quit smoking?" he asked. My father was unable to answer the question honestly. He could not admit he had failed again, and so he lied to my uncle. "Yes," he answered, "I gave myself a Christmas present. I have quit smoking." He knew that his brother did not believe him. My uncle could smell smoke all over his clothes and on his breath. There was no way to hide it. With pretended enthusiasm and congratulations, my uncle told him how happy he was that the effort was over and he had quit. They both knew they were lying.

The day was dismal without Christmas cheer. My father left early to return home. He called us to exchange the normal Christmas greetings, then slumped in a chair with his hated cigarettes. He had reached a low in his life. All hope was gone. He could not conquer the habit. He had broken his promise to his Father in Heaven, to his granddaughter, and to himself. He had lied to his brother. He would not be able to return to the temple, and there was no one left to help him.

At this great moment of despair he went into his bedroom, got on his knees, and begged God for an answer. He told his Father in Heaven that it was beyond his power to quit smoking. He had changed his life in every other way, but he was chained to cigarettes, and no power on earth could break those chains, if God didn't intervene. He pleaded with his Father in Heaven to help him so he could go back to the temple and be a father to his children and a grandfather to his grandchildren. For a long time he stayed on his knees, and when he was exhausted he went to bed. But he felt a peace that brought immediate sleep.

He woke up the next morning and looked at the cigarettes on the nightstand. Something had happened in the night while he slept. God had given him his Christmas present. The desire to smoke was gone. Furthermore, it never returned. In its place was an aversion to tobacco. But it was more than that. It was my father's answer, the one he had sought all his life, the assurance that the greatest Father of all loved his child enough to help him conquer the effects of his own life's disobedience. It was the promise that as long as we call God "Father," there will always be hope, no matter how far we drift nor how long we linger near the precipice.

There is a deep beauty in that love and in the hope it gives us all. Somewhere in the eternal worlds there must be a name for it, though I do not know it. I have felt it in my life and know its power in the life of my earthly father. It is more than love. It is a holiness that makes the title Father in Heaven the only name sacred enough to give Deity. But all of this was unknown to me that Christmas of 1983.

In February of 1984 the telephone rang. It was my father. He was jubilant.

I had never heard his voice ring with such joy. "Do you know what I'm holding in my hand?" he asked. "It is a temple recommend. I am worthy. I have won the battle. I have received my answer. Will you come to Salt Lake City and go through the temple with me? I have not been there since I knelt across the altar with your mother over thirty years ago."

On March 17, 1984, my wife and I flew to Salt Lake and walked through the temple doors with my father. As we sat in the celestial room I thought of the miracle of the Atonement and I remembered the words of my favorite scripture when Jesus said: "I have set before thee an open door, and no man can shut it." My father was walking through that door.

BENEATH MY BIRTHDAY TREE

Brad Wilcox

Being born on Christmas
Is quite unique because,
You never know who brought you —
The stork or Santa Claus.

I was born on December 25. One year my cousins gave me that little verse in a Christmas card — or was it a birthday card? When people find out I was born on Christmas Day, they usually don't believe me, so I have to dig out my driver's license to prove it. Or they moan and say, "How terrible!"

"What's terrible — that I was born?"

"No, that you were born on Christmas."

For some reason, I've always looked at it as an honor. Every year my parents hung up a banner that read, "Happy Birthday to Jesus and Brad." My Grandma Camenish used to remind me that Joseph Smith was born at Christmastime, too — on December 23. Between the Lord and the Prophet, I felt I was in good company. In fact, I still remember my disappointment when some Sunday School teacher taught us that the Savior was actually born in April.

Still, well-meaning friends think it's tragic to be born on the biggest holiday of the year. "After all," they sympathize, "you probably don't even get any birthday gifts."

That's true. Usually, whatever present anyone had for me was simply given with a "Merry Birthday" card to cover both occasions — that is, until my wise and wonderful parents came up with the Birthday Tree.

In our home, as I grew up, we simply put up two trees — one for Christmas and one for my birthday. My cousins and brothers then had to put a gift for me under each tree. It worked great until one year when my brother, Roger, bought me a pair of mittens. He wrapped one and put it under the Christmas tree, and the other he put under the Birthday Tree. I personally put a chunk of coal in his stocking the next morning.

Even now, my own children enjoy carrying on the tradition. Each December, we find space in our little home for two trees. Wendee and Russell glow as brightly as any electric lights or tinsel star when we start pulling out the hodge-

19

podge ornaments we've collected. Then we decorate the trees—one for Jesus, and one for Daddy.

As young as my children are, they know the gifts that come from neighborhood and ward friends go beneath the Christmas tree. But the special gifts—the ones just for Daddy—go beneath the Birthday Tree. One of those gifts particularly stands out in my memory.

It was the weekend right before Christmas. As with many of the previous weekends, I was spending this one away from home. I had been in southern California for several days speaking to youth groups. I had spoken of Christ, his birth and mission, the Restoration, and his living prophets on earth today.

After my last talk, I said good-bye quickly to my new friends because I simply could not miss my plane. I had to be back in Utah that same evening for another commitment.

Just as I was heading out the chapel door, one young man stepped forward. "Brother Wilcox, do you remember my brother? You met him with me last summer." Tears started brimming. "Well, he remembers you. But he didn't come tonight because he has gotten in with the wrong kids at school and . . . " The tears fell. Through his sobs, we spoke of his brother's inactivity in the Church. He expressed concern over his brother's poor choices and darkened countenance. "If you could just see him," he suggested. "I know he remembers you. Could you just

come by our house on your way to the airport?" What else could I do?

Soon I was standing before a struggling young man who was feeling a lot of things—and the Christmas spirit was not one of them. "Hey, my buddy," I offered, "let's go for a walk."

We circled the block again and again. Our talk lasted longer than it takes to sing "The Twelve Days of Christmas" twenty-four times. Promises were made. Hearts were lightened. Love was expressed.

"Thanks," both brothers offered together.

"No problem," I smiled. Then I climbed back in the car, looked at my watch, and realized that there was indeed a problem. More rapid than eagles my course I flew. But I arrived at the local airport too late and ended up missing my sleigh. "When's the next flight?" I asked.

"No more flights," the attendant said mechanically.

"No more flights?" I said, panicking.

She probably wanted to say, "Isn't that what I just said?" But she restrained herself. After all, it was Christmastime. Automatically, she typed several things into her computer and stated, "The next available flight to Salt Lake leaves from LAX."

"LAX?" I repeated again.

She glared.

"That's too far away. I have to get home tonight—I must!"

She checked her computer again, shook her head, and shrugged. There was nothing else to do. Quickly I rented a car again and started towards Los Angeles, all the while singing, "All I want for Christmas is a clear freeway."

I arrived at that huge airport with only minutes to spare. There was no time to check bags—including gifts I had chosen for my family. I was loaded up as high as the missionaries' plates when they come for Christmas dinner.

The uniformed agent was already closing the door when I came panting up to the gate. "Please," I said, hyperventilating, "I've got to get on that plane!"

"But sir . . . " She started to tell me there was no room in the inn. Then, looking at what must have been a pitiful sight, this kind innkeeper lead me to the stable. Latches were undone. Doors were opened. Other travelers questioned what was causing the delay. When what to their wondering eyes should appear? Brad Wilcox, completely buried under Christmas packages and suitcases.

I waded between the front few seats and dove for the first empty spot. Once planted, I exhaled loudly. The good man right next to me offered, "Can I help you with some of those things?" It was Elder Gene R. Cook of the First Quorum of the Seventy. He smiled, "I'm glad you made it."

"Thanks," I managed. I felt as awkward as outdoor Christmas lights in March. Elder Cook helped me get settled, and we began to talk.

He asked, "Did you see who you passed up there?"

"No, who?"

"The prophet is sitting right up there with his wife."

I couldn't speak. With my luck, I'd probably just hit him with my luggage. I could see the headlines in the *Church News*: "Brad Wilcox Bashes Prophet with Hanging Suit Bag." I felt terrible.

Elder Cook went on. "He was here for a special regional meeting we just concluded. He is sitting right up there with his wife and Elder Boyd K. Packer of the Quorum of the Twelve."

"Really?" I was getting excited. I had just quoted Elder Packer in the talk I gave to the young people. My spirit tingled. I felt as if someone were pouring a little holiday 7–Up all through me. I love the Brethren. I study their words and try to pattern my life after their examples. But such closeness to them is a rarity for me.

Here I was, sitting right next to a humble representative of the Savior. Here I was within rows of men I sustain with all my heart as prophets, seers, and revelators—"teachers of the known truth . . . perceivers of hidden truth . . . and bearers of new truth." (John A. Widtsoe, *Evidences and Reconciliations*, comp. G. Homer Durham [Salt Lake City: Bookcraft, 1960], pages 257–58.)

The flight attendant offered me some juice. I didn't want anything. I just pulled out my journal in hopes of recording some of the thoughts and feelings that were bubbling inside me.

"Excuse me," said Elder Packer, who now stood next to my aisle seat. Elder

Cook moved toward the window, and I stood to let Elder Packer sit down next to him. They talked softly together.

I thought I was writing in my journal the entire time. But looking back at the pages now, there is really nothing there. One would suppose that empty journal pages could not communicate much. However, these particular blank pages express more than enough to me.

I had just quoted the apostle who sat next to me. I had just read his words to the young people: "I have heard his voice and received a witness, even a special witness of him. I pray God that each of us this Christmas will at last open [Christ's] gift and discover who *we* are, and who *he* is." (*A Christmas Parable* [Salt Lake City: Bookcraft, 1986], page 13.)

Elder Packer suddenly turned toward me. "Well, Brad, Elder Cook tells me you have been here addressing the youth."

I nodded.

"What did you tell them?" he asked politely.

"Elder Packer," I spoke quietly, "I told them about you. I bore testimony that you are an apostle—just as Peter, James, and John were apostles. I bore my testimony of living prophets. I bore my witness of you."

Elder Packer sat thoughtfully for a moment. Then, smiling at Elder Cook and back at me, he said, "If you're going to go running around saying things like that, I guess I'd better try to do a little better."

We spoke for several more minutes,

and then Elder Packer returned to his seat. I looked across the now-empty chair between us and caught Elder Cook's eyes.

"Thank you for saying something to him."

Elder Cook raised his eyebrows as if to say, "Who, me?"

"Yes, you," I said. I knew that Elder Cook had to have whispered something to Elder Packer about the guy behind him named Brad who was having a near cardiac arrest. Elder Cook will never know what a treasured moment that was for me. "Thank you," I spoke again.

Elder Cook simply smiled, "Merry Christmas, Brad."

God has given the world wonderful gifts. He gave us Christ, the Atonement, the Resurrection, and the Restoration. He gives us the gift of the Holy Ghost when we qualify for it, temples, the Book of Mormon, priesthood authority, and living prophets. But on that particular Christmas, I felt I had received something more. The opportunity for me to be that close to the living prophet, to meet Elder Packer and Elder Cook, and feel the spiritual witness that came on that occasion seemed extra somehow.

In a world where, in too many cases, Christ himself has become nothing more than a Christmas decoration, I appreciate those who stand as his authorized servants. The Savior must not become something we bring out of the closet once a year to sing about, talk about, and ultimately pack away until next December. We must follow Christ daily, by following his special witnesses.

Jesus is no longer a babe we read about in a manger, and he is no longer a crucified body in the tomb. Christ is a fully grown man who lives today. He directs us now, as he always has, through the words of living prophets and apostles. Their words give me security and peace. Their testimonies give evidence for my faith. Their eyes give me light to follow.

President Harold B. Lee once wrote, "That person is not truly converted un-til he sees the power of God resting upon the leaders of this church, and until it goes down into his heart like fire." ("The Strength of the Priesthood," *Ensign*, July 1972.) I have now felt that fire. I do not simply march to the beat of a different drummer. I follow *the* drummers who follow the Savior.

This personal testimony was a gift. It was not just another Christmas present to be piled with the others under the Christmas tree. Rather, this was a special gift, placed—very personally, it seemed to me—beneath my Birthday Tree.

FRIENDSHIP'S GIFT

Arthur S. Anderson

It looked like a scene from the latest war movie. Except this time I was in the cast—one of the extras. Or so it seemed as I stood in a long line of soldiers climbing slowly up the gangplank with duffle bags slung across their backs. The silence was deathly. It was midnight in early August of 1945 at a San Francisco military port of embarkation. Our departure was taking place under cover of darkness as a precaution against enemy submarines that could be lurking in the off-shore waters.

For the first time in three years of Army service, I felt alone in a crowd. Doubtless most others in the military had experienced that feeling many times. But I had been spoiled by a series of fortunate coincidences.

The draft had caught up with our entire University of Utah junior class ROTC unit at the same time. We went to basic training at Camp Roberts, California, together and saw friends every day. At night the regimental recreation room was a gathering place for writing letters home and comparing notes to see whose drill sergeant had the loudest bark.

When the opportunity came to attend artillery officers candidate school, my brother, Warren, just a year-and-a-half my senior, was next to me alphabetically and we were assigned to the same four-man hut at school in Fort Sill, Oklahoma. We stayed together for nearly a year-and-a-half before our orders took us in opposite directions.

Now as I climbed aboard that troop carrier in silence, every sign of previous acquaintance was gone. I tossed my bag on the first bunk inside the large dormitory-type room filled with double-decker beds and settled down for a long ride that everyone sensed would end with combat troops making the initial attack on the main island of Japan.

As it happened, midway in our journey across the Pacific Ocean, the atomic bomb was dropped on Hiroshima and news of the Japanese surrender came with the most excited "now hear this" preface I had ever heard.

In a twinkling, life changed from death-threatening to the prospect of an organized and hopefully peaceful occupation of the mystery land of Japan.

As a battalion of the 81st Infantry Division, we were the first troops sent onto the far north end of Honshu, the main island. The barracks were austere, made of tinder-box dry wood with no reliable electricity and no means of heating. The weather was similar to that found in the northern United States, with plenty of snow and an average five months of winter.

Of course, there was much to be thankful for, but with the war over, the cause won, my longings for home, friends, family, and getting on with life were stronger than ever.

As Christmas approached that year, the feeling of being alone in a crowd returned; and although I had spent three previous Christmases away from home, this one seemed destined to be especially lonely.

How I longed to see a familiar face, to talk about home with someone who could share the feelings of Christmas in Salt Lake City, the friendly people in the neighborhood and the ward, the *Messiah* sung in the Tabernacle, and family together around the fire.

My requests for a short leave had apparently gone unheeded, so when I woke up on December 24, all hope of getting to Tokyo, some five hundred miles away, was gone. There would be a gathering of friends from the University ROTC group in Tokyo on Christmas, and how I longed to be there! Keith Engar would be flying in from Okinawa. Burton Brasher had extra beds in the Matsu Motoro Restaurant in

the block next to the Imperial Palace, which had been converted into officer living quarters.

Then came a phone call from Frank McKean, a college friend who, to my surprise, was working in division headquarters. He had found my travel request just hours before and, knowing that travel requests to visit Tokyo were never approved, arranged for my assignment to a rest and recuperation retreat near Mount Fuji. Tokyo was enroute.

By noon I was on the train. I traveled all night, arriving in Tokyo at noon on Christmas Day. What a happy reunion! Nobody thought of presents or even much about what was for dinner. It was so heartwarming to be together with friends and share feelings of home.

Who would have guessed that by evening we would all be seated together in a large concert hall in the center of Tokyo. The Japanese Philharmonic and a combined American and Japanese Christian chorus with the best national soloists gave the most thrilling rendition of the *Messiah* that I shall ever hear. As the sounds of the "Hallelujah Chorus" rang out and all rose reverently to their feet, I looked down the row at treasured friends: on the left, Burton Brasher, Wally Bennett, Ken Sundwall, Dick Clawson, Croft, and Dave Smith. More on the right—Keith Engar, Verl Scott, Bill Pope, and Harold Sutherland. It was a scene indelibly engraved. Then I turned to the stage where Japanese and Americans stood together in common love for the author of Peace on Earth.

No one wishes for the contrast of war so as to have a full appreciation of peace. No one wishes to be lonely to get the full impact of being unexpectedly with dear friends. No one wishes for time away from family and friends to appreciate the things that are the most important in life. But as the strains of the chorus and symphony rose to the final crescendo, a consciousness of the true meaning of Christmas filled my whole being.

Forty-five Christmases have come and gone since then, but it is doubtful there will ever be another Christmas quite like 1945.

RINGS OF GROWTH

Elaine L. Jack

Every Christmas I envision the bushy, fragrant pine trees we had in my parents' home in Canada. My dad had a friend who cut one fresh from the nearby mountains and hauled it to our home on a horse-drawn sleigh. These huge trees brushed the ceiling and filled the corner of our living room with branches heavy enough to hold our wrapped presents. From those earliest days, the Christmas tree has represented to me everything good about the season: my home, the love we share, family togetherness, and Christmas itself.

It was exciting to be a bride living in Staten Island, New York, during the Christmas season of 1949. Both my husband, Joe, and I worked in Manhattan and spent our limited time together happily exploring the city. We were having a wonderful time. Life was good.

Early in December we received a letter from Fred, an old neighborhood friend of Joe's, telling us that he would be in New York for three days on his way home from a two-year mission. We knew that he had served in Czechoslo-

vakia for eighteen months and had completed his mission in England, but we were oblivious to the conditions in Europe at that time. We were light-hearted, carefree, and eager to share our Christmas cheer with an old friend.

Fred arrived a sobered young missionary. He told us of being forcibly expelled from Czechoslovakia, of scarce food, of dwindling medical supplies in the country, of the devotion of the Latter-day Saints, and about how he hated to leave them. He was unsettled and troubled by the oppressive events he had witnessed in Europe.

It was two weeks before Christmas. While I was preparing a special turkey dinner the evening after he arrived, I suggested that Joe and Fred go on the bus to get a Christmas tree for the bedroom of our small, two-room apartment. I was anxious to have a tree. While Joe and Fred were gone, I envisioned a beautiful, full tree, reminiscent of those we'd had back home.

When I heard Joe and Fred coming up the stairs, I rushed to see what they had brought. Joe held the New York version of a Christmas tree—small enough to be carried in one hand. I was shocked! This Christmas tree would never do. "It will be just fine for the table," Joe said. A tree that would fit on a table? A table tree was simply not acceptable! I pointed out the only solution, "Take it back and get a bigger one." Joe must have sensed how important it was to me, because with minimal protesting he and Fred took the small tree back on the bus to exchange if for a larger one.

The six-foot tree with sparse branches and short needles that he and Fred brought back ended up at the foot of our bed. It wasn't very beautiful, even with decorations, but at least it was a tree which could bridge the transition from the Christmases of the past to the establishing of our own family memories and traditions.

Seven years later our home was in southeast Alaska. Joe and I and our first two sons, David, six, and Bill, four, lived in government housing at the edge of a large area of muskeg—a spongy, swampy bog covered with moss and plants. Ponds of water, a few pine trees, small shrubs, and skunk cabbage were scattered across this fertile area.

Because they stood alone, muskeg pine trees were usually well formed and symmetrical—perfect for Christmas trees. One afternoon close to Christmas we decided to create a family tradition by chopping our own fresh Christmas tree.

We took an axe and a saw and walked to the edge of the muskeg,

squishing through the tundra. We examined each tree along the way. Finally, some distance into the bog, we found the perfect one. Joe hacked off the lower branches so he could reach the thick trunk with the saw. Dave, Bill, and I held branches out of the way while he worked at felling the tree. When it toppled over, we were delighted. Dragging the tree and walking was too much for the boys, so we went on ahead, carefully picking our footing while Joe pulled the tree by himself through the thick, goopy bog.

When next I looked, Joe was stranded in the soggiest part of the muskeg, which oozed around the top of his boots. As he tried to pull one foot onto solid ground, he succeeded only in burying the other foot deeper into the muck. No matter which foot he tried to extract, he sank further. He couldn't find a solid base anywhere. And to our horror, he was slowly sinking into the ground!

"Stay where you are, kids," I instructed. "I'm going to help Dad." Joe yelled, "Stay back! I'll catch my breath and get out of this." Fortunately, the branches of the bushy tree had spread over the marshy area; Joe braced himself on the branches and struggled to firmer ground. He was exhausted. With the last of his energy, he pulled the tree to the edge of the muskeg and left it there until he could borrow a truck to transport it the rest of the way to our house.

It had been a harrowing experience, but what a tree we had! It was exactly the kind you might see in City Hall.

When we got home, we could hardly pull it through the door. Although that tree hadn't filled much of the muskeg, it bumped against the ceiling and nearly touched all four walls of our living room. We chopped off branches from the back of the tree, shoved it toward the corner, then hacked off more branches until it was finally stuffed into the space where it belonged. The lopsided tree fit perfectly with the help of wires to hold it up. We have never had a more magnificent tree. Nor have I ever had a more fatigued husband. Afterwards, Joe said simply, "In the future, whatever price you have to pay for a tree, pay it. It is worth it!"

Much as I love fragrant, green trees, I followed the fashion in the early sixties and decided to flock our tree. I thought the natural look of a tree after a snowstorm would be a wonderful addition to our Christmas decor. With a do-it-yourself flocking kit that attached to my vacuum cleaner, I was sure I could create a beautiful tree for much less than a flocked tree cost right off the lot. I decided to do the job where the tree would stand so none of the flocking would be disturbed. I connected the vacuum to the powdery flocking material and the bottle of water and turned on the power. It worked! Synthetic snow made the tree look like a winter wonderland. As I finished and stepped back to admire my Currier and Ives tree, I noticed that the wall, the sofa, the piano, and chairs were also part of

my winter wonderland. We had a spectacular tree, but snow removal that year continued into June. The following year I remembered Joe's advice given years earlier in Alaska and paid the price for a tree someone else had flocked.

Last year I didn't send Joe for a tree; I didn't flock one myself; I didn't even buy a Christmas tree. Our children have moved to homes of their own, and I used other decorations to bring the festive feelings of Christmas into our home. It was a different kind of Christmas for me. Even without a tree, the feelings that Christmas trees symbolize seemed more real to me than ever before. I basked in the warmth created by years of family togetherness around our trees.

A thousand memories fill my heart at Christmastime — memories that have grown and matured into a deeper understanding that the peace and goodwill brought to earth with the birth of the Savior are the basis for all the good and wonderful things Christmas represents. I reflected upon the New York "return-the-tree" season of 1949 and thought how blessed we were to have had the luxury of worrying about the size of our tree when so many people had no means at all. I remembered my two little boys, now fathers, and laughed about Joe's skirmish with a muskeg bog in Alaska. I thought about the many fashions of the holidays. And while flocked trees, like wide collars, come and go, the spirit and meaning of Christmas do not change.

CHRISTMAS REFLECTIONS

Stephen M. Studdert

As I reflect on Christmas memories, two special Christmas seasons nearly ten years apart are inseparably linked in my memory. The year of 1981 had dawned bright as springtime blossomed across Poland with a renewed dream of hope and freedom for the struggling Polish people. As the fledgling but spirited Solidarity Movement, known to the Poles as *Solidarnose*, began to grow, the thoughts of long-fought-for freedoms filled the hearts and desires of fathers and mothers and children across that repressed land.

It ended abruptly a few short days before Christmas of that year as the darkness of totalitarianism spread across Poland for the third time in the twentieth century. Christmas in Poland was celebrated not with peace and joy and goodwill toward all men, but tragically in violence and death and bitter repression.

Across the cold, windswept, snowy Polish countryside, in the small impoverished villages and the large industrial cities, iron tanks rumbled to a stop and the quest for freedom was quickly crushed.

As our family, like families across America and the free lands of the world, gathered happily together near a warm hearth and freely sang the carols of Christmas, a gentle, brave Polish electrician named Lech Walesa also gathered his family together.

In an apartment cold and cramped but filled with their love of Christ, together they offered a brief and silent prayer. Surrounded by trial and fear, yet with abiding faith in a caring Savior of all mankind, they offered a sincere plea for his help.

With love and tenderness, this devoted and faithful father kissed his courageous wife and each of his six frightened children good-bye as he was taken away by the dreaded secret police into the darkness of the night to a destination and a destiny unknown.

Communications between Poland and the outside world were severed. The Solidarity Movement, which had quickly embraced the people and the spirit of the Polish nation, was outlawed. And again, almost overnight, the people of Poland became a nation imprisoned.

But the dream of freedom was still alive in Poland. With bold silence, Christmas candles began to light the windows of Poland's houses and communes. These were simple, individual, yet powerful statements of the love of liberty burning bright in the hearts of a courageous people.

That Christmas Eve of 1981, another man who also loved freedom and liberty lighted a solidarity candle. Ronald Reagan, President of the United States, lit a small but purposeful candle that burned silently through the darkness of the night in an upper window of the White House. Like others across America, it burned in solidarity with the Polish people.

The previous spring, Ronald Reagan had been recovering from an assassination attempt. He had made his first outing outside of Washington to accept an honorary degree from the University of Notre Dame. It was a deeply touching moment for those of us with him as we remembered how close to death's door he had come, and now saw and felt the outpouring of affection from that cheering student body and their families.

But Ronald Reagan was not the only person to receive an honorary degree from Notre Dame. The following spring another recipient was the Polish electrician and proponent of freedom, Lech Walesa. Of course, Lech was still in prison, his fate unknown, and he was obviously unable to come to the United States to accept that deserved degree.

And so at Notre Dame that stage held a single unfilled place, an empty chair, bearing only the Solidarity banner, awaiting the release of Lech Walesa and the liberation of the Polish people.

The crowd stood and cheered for five tumultuous minutes in honor of the empty chair and the man who wasn't there, a tribute to freedom and individual courage.

Years later, as the brilliance of fall in America's capitol city faded quietly into winter with the Christmas season of 1989 approaching, I sat in the majestic East Room of the White House. On the platform stood another President and another empty chair. George Bush, with tears in his eyes, told Lech Walesa to "take your place in this house of freedom. Take your place in the empty chair."

As a hundred or so of us stood cheering and were filled with emotion, the President of the United Stated conferred America's highest civilian honor, the Medal of Freedom, on this common man who loves freedom and who was willing to pay any price to enjoy in some small measure what we sometimes take for granted.

The nights lengthened, the days grew colder, and Christmas came. Our family gathered around a large, comforting fire on Christmas Eve, safe and secure, and thankful for religious freedom and personal liberty. Following our annual family tradition, we read aloud from Luke the story of the glorious birth of the Savior of all mankind. "For unto you is born this day in the city of David a Saviour, which is Christ the Lord."

The Prince of Peace. Born in a stable for there was no room in the inn. Silently my thoughts were drawn back to that humble citizen of Poland, Lech Walesa, his family, and their lonely Christmas of 1981. I recalled the words of the Book of Mormon, "The Spirit of God . . . is also the spirit of freedom" (Alma 61:15). And we read together, "And suddenly there was with the angel a multitude of the heavenly host praising God, and saying, Glory to God in the highest, and on earth peace, good will toward men" (Luke 2:13–14).

With grateful hearts we offered our prayer for his peace for all the world.

MY HEART SANG A LULLABY

Janice Kapp Perry

As I have experienced fifty Christmas seasons in my life, one might think it would be difficult to recall the most memorable of these happy times. However, for me the choice can easily be narrowed to two unique Christmas experiences that occurred nearly twenty years apart. Each involved a newborn baby—somehow so appropriate and exciting at Christmastime—and yet each evoked such opposite, never-to-be-forgotten feelings of love.

December 1968

As struggling graduate students at Indiana University, my husband, Doug, and I were looking forward to a rather bleak prospect of Christmas gift-giving. We were, however, feeling much excitement at the expected arrival of our fifth child.

Then just days before Christmas a routine pregnancy blood test revealed that our baby was in serious trauma from the effects of the Rh-factor, and probably would not survive long without drastic measures being initiated. Since Doug was at work, some two hours from home, and time was critical,

friends in the Church took our four children into their homes while our Relief Society president drove me sixty miles to the Indianapolis Medical Center. There the doctors tested amniotic fluid and made the decision to perform an intrauterine transfusion—a tedious procedure in which a needle is inserted through the mother's abdomen so that whole blood plasma can be transfused into the baby's abdomen over a period of a few hours. It is hoped that this healthy plasma will sustain the baby's life until birth.

The procedure seemed to be successful, but the next morning, on Sunday, as Doug and I were talking in our hospital room, my labor started prematurely. After a difficult day of labor and many prayers for our baby, a three-and-one-half-pound baby boy was born to us at eight o'clock that evening. We were comforted to hear his cries as he was born, but at that point we didn't know if he would live. He was extremely ill, and doctors took him from us quickly to perform blood exchanges and other life-saving measures.

When everything possible had been

done for him medically, Doug placed his hands on the baby's head in the tiny incubator and gave him the name of Richard Scott Perry as well as a powerful but loving father's blessing. Then we watched and prayed through the night.

At five o'clock the next morning, Richard died. Doug wrapped him in a tiny white blanket and brought him to my hospital room where we held him and loved him and prayed for comfort through our tears. It's a moment engraved in both our memories, a time when for both of us the words "born under the covenant" came to have new meaning.

I stayed in the hospital to rest one more day. Doug returned home to Bloomington where he gathered our four children together for a special home evening to tell the story of a little baby who only needed to live on earth briefly but who would always be a very real part of our eternal family.

Christmas feelings and festivities were in full swing all around us as I returned home. But I felt as though I were observing everything from a distance. Different things mattered to me this year. Friends came by to offer sympathy and support, and some even brought gifts. But for perhaps the first time in my life I experienced Christmas as I feel sure it was meant to be felt — caring nothing for the commercial aspects of the season but feeling a deep and abiding appreciation and love for my children and husband and the gifts of the Spirit. The world seemed

changed to me — eternity's promise seemed so much clearer, and I wanted only to bask in the new insights this tender event had caused me to have.

Christmas morning was peaceful and good. Relatives from Utah and Illinois had sent gifts for the children, and Doug and I watched as they happily discovered them. As for me, I remember most vividly a thoughtful gift from my lifelong best friend. It had come in the mail a few days earlier with the instruction "to be opened Christmas morning." As I carefully untied the ribbon, I felt gratitude for a thoughtful friend who, though we normally didn't exchange Christmas gifts, was sensitive to my unique need that Christmas. Inside the package was a beautiful, long, crimson velvet robe and a book dealing with eternal life. In her familiar handwriting she had written, "After the children have opened their Christmas gifts and you've spent some time with them, try to find some time alone, put on this robe, and read from this book. You will find peace and reassurance there regarding your little son. Love, Delma."

I did as she suggested, reading for many hours and having confirmed all of the feelings of hope and peace that had filled me ever since Richard's birth. Just as anciently one baby's coming had changed the course of the world, our baby's coming had changed *us* forever in a very real way. It had given us new sensitivity and understanding, new experience with the Comforter, and new determination to live worthy to someday be where Richard surely is.

Every year as the first Christmas music of the season is played—and that's usually very early in our home—this unique Christmas memory returns and we are all touched again in a beautiful way by our memories of Richard.

Years later, when it had become so natural for me to write songs about important life events, I carefully relived the details of our experience with Richard in writing the song "My Heart Sang a Lullaby." Now I have only to sing this lullaby whenever I want to remember the feelings of that time.

My Heart Sang a Lullaby

Richie was born on a day in December.
I know it was Sunday—some things
    you remember.
Richie's first cries were like music to
    me,
But no one could promise how long he
    would stay.
And the night seemed so long as we
    watched him and prayed.

Chorus:
And my heart sang a lullaby to cele-
    brate birth,
As he crossed the veil between heaven
    and earth.
My heart sang a lullaby for this tiny
    one,
A song of forever, of things yet to
    come,
Just a lullaby to carry him home.

Richie was gone by the light of the
    morning,
Before his first sunrise, before the day's
    dawning.

So still in our arms, it was our turn to
    cry,
A memorized moment as we said good-
    bye.
And he looked like an angel in his blan-
    ket of white.

(Repeat Chorus)

Richie, my son, only here for a mo-
    ment,
He came and he went and the world
    didn't notice.
But nothing's the same, especially for
    me;
Eternity's promise is clearer to see.
He has just gone ahead to where we'll
    someday be.

(Repeat Chorus)

Just a lullaby to carry him home.
Just a lullaby to carry him home.

December 1987

Nearly twenty years had passed since Richie's death. Although we had hoped to have a larger family, it was not possible for us to bear any more children after the effects of Rh-factor had become so severe. Foster children and puppies helped to fill the empty spaces for us.

Imagine our joy when we learned that our first grandchild was due to be born Christmas Day of 1987! Of course, babies rarely arrive on their due date, but just anticipating a baby in the Christmas season was exciting.

We watched anxiously as the weeks and months passed, leading to this new season of life for us. We were more than ready to be grandparents, and looked upon this event as the ultimate Christmas gift—a kind of compensation for our loss years ago.

When Christmas Eve came and went with no signs of an imminent birth, and after the doctor said to the expectant mother, "We'll check you again in a week," we all settled in for the wait. But then *the call* came at seven o'clock Christmas morning. "Mom, we're at the hospital and they're not sending us home!"

Instantly, this Christmas held an excitement unequalled by any Christmas past. Robb promised to call us with progress reports throughout the day, and we gamely tried to proceed with our usual Christmas morning routine. But we were all so excited that we could hardly open gifts in any sane fashion. Each phone call from the hospital sent the adrenaline pumping, and the final call at three o'clock in the afternoon announcing the arrival of Jessica Noelle Perry was a moment of indescribable happiness for us. (We knew they would name a daughter Jessica, but Noelle was added because of her timely Christmas arrival.)

We quickly drove across town to the hospital, and raced to the nursery for our first view of Jessica. This new grandma could not restrain the tears as we first saw her through the nursery window, *au naturale,* kicking and crying and looking strangely familiar. I was truly in awe of the whole experience.

Later as she was placed in my arms, wrapped in a white blanket, the years melted away in my mind. This was the first time since Richie's death that I had held a newborn and felt complete joy.

Our granddaughter's name—Jessica Noelle—was a song title if ever I had heard one. I began forming lyrics for a Christmas calypso by that title.

Jessica Noelle

One Christmas morning we still recall,
Came to us the best gift of all,
Our son called early that joyous morn
To say our first grandchild would be
    born.
We opened presents from Santa Claus,
Light with laughter and joy because
We were waiting so happily, wond'ring
    who the baby would be.
And she was

Chorus:
Jessica Noelle, Christmas angel from
    heaven fell,
Jessica Noelle, a Christmas story we
    love to tell,
Light the Christmas tree, ring the bell,
Welcome little Jessie Noelle.

We traveled quickly that wintry day,
To the place where the baby lay,
We looked in wonder, we gazed in awe
At the little stranger we saw.
They placed the baby within our arms,
Tears were falling now, soft and warm,
No one can measure, no words can tell
Of the perfect love that we felt.
As we held

(Repeat Chorus)

Our Christmas angel was born to earth
The day we celebrate Jesus' birth,

And through the years we will all recall
The most merry Christmas of all,
With little

(Repeat Chorus)

Light the Christmas tree, ring the bell,
Welcome little Jessie Noelle.

Some of my happiest and most poignant Christmas memories will forever be tied closely to babies. Some have expressed the hope that no one close to them would ever die during the Christmas season because the holidays would forever hold such painful memories.

For me, it has seemed the perfect time to remember a soul-touching event that was bittersweet at the time but which, with the perspective of time and teaching by the Spirit, has become only sweet and edifying.

How grateful we are for Richie, who in his short life taught us about life, death, eternal ties, and trust in the Lord's timing!

And how dearly we love Jessica Noelle, our sweet Christmas baby, for the sunshine and promise she brings to our present.

CHRISTMAS WITH A PROPHET

D. Arthur Haycock

The following is an excerpt from the personal journal of President George Albert Smith, the eighth President of The Church of Jesus Christ of Latter-day Saints:

"*Friday, December 24, 1948*: Salt Lake City. Snow.

"The office was closed, but I came down early in order to clear a number of matters from my desk. I worked at the office until shortly after noon, with Arthur helping me. We then had a bite of lunch before making some visits. Went to the Primary Children's Hospital (situated directly across the street from the North Temple entrance to the temple grounds) and visited all the little children, presenting books and wishing them a Merry Christmas. Went to the L.D.S. Hospital to see Sister Alice Smoot. My daughter, Edith Elliott, then joined me and we visited Evelyn Woodruff, and Mrs. Alice Strong, where Arthur helped me administer to her. I also called on Flora Sears and Florence Critchlow. Returned home in the late afternoon for a quiet Christmas Eve with my family."

The above represents just a brief out-

line of President Smith's activities that day. I was with him during the entire day until he finally went home in the evening to rest and be with his family. I was privileged to be present as he went from place to place, ministering to young and old.

At the Primary Children's Hospital we attended the program portraying the birth of the baby Jesus in a stable in Bethlehem, as it was presented by the little children who were patients in that place of love and healing. Joseph was played by a little boy on crutches; Mary was a beautiful little girl in a wheelchair who held a doll "wrapped in swaddling clothes." As she looked down tenderly and lovingly into the face of the doll, I am sure that even angels would have been moved to tears. Certainly we were. The three wise men, dressed in long hospital gowns, and their heads wrapped in brightly colored towels, were there to pay homage and present their gifts of gold, frankincense, and myrrh. They, too, were on crutches or in wheelchairs.

With the Lord's prophet there present, I have often wondered if this blessed event was ever reenacted with more sincerity, love and faith than that which we witnessed as each little sick or crippled child did his or her part. Afterward, President Smith visited each child in his bed or wheel chair and gave them a children's book and a shining new silver coin as a remembrance. Many of them asked for, and received, a blessing. As we left the hospital, all the children shouted, "Merry Christmas, President Smith." Although each little one was suffering from a serious ailment or handicap, they displayed wonderful Christlike love, faith and innocence.

Following our visit to the Primary Children's Hospital and the L.D.S. Hospital we drove to the Salt Lake County Hospital infirmary to wish those lonely and oft-forgotten elderly patients a Merry Christmas. What a sad and heart-breaking sight they were! In the separate men's and women's wards there were row after row of iron beds lined up on the bare floor. The walls were gray and bare, and there were no curtains at the windows.

Many appeared to be the "living dead," for the most part almost abandoned or forgotten by their own families. They were not, however, forgotten by the prophet of the Lord. President Smith commented, "Isn't it strange that one mother can take care of ten children, but ten children can't seem to take care of one mother who has grown old and sick and worn!" We went from bed to bed, with the President visiting personally with each one and blessing

those who asked. Christmas was brightened for those in that hospital by a visit from the Lord's servant.

This is just a glimpse of one day in the life of President George Albert Smith, as I was privileged to see it during the years I served as his personal secretary. But it wasn't just during the holidays that President Smith expressed love and kindness to one and all. His life and teachings were based completely on the two great commandments given by the Lord: love of God and love of neighbor. In a talk given in 1943 he said: "Let us love one another. If there ever was a time when we needed to be kind, it is now. If there ever was a time when we needed to be patient, it is now; and if we would keep one of the commandments of God that He said was second to the greatest, we will love our neighbors as ourselves."

President Smith was especially thoughtful of the children of Father Lehi (as he always referred to the Indians and Polynesians), the handicapped, the deaf and the blind. In my den at home I have hanging on the wall the original of a tribute given President Smith, entitled "The Understanding Heart." The author was a blind woman, Irene Jones, who, at the request of his family, read the following at his funeral held in the Tabernacle:

When life beats hard with stormy
    hands
And bitter teardrops fall,
When friendless winter chills my soul
And empty echoes call,

'Tis then I turn with eager hope,
My steps though spent and lame,
To find an understanding heart
Where burns a friendly flame.
A heart where gentle wisdom dwells,
Compassionate and kind;
Where faith in God and man has
    taught,
A like faith to the blind.
I lay my troubles at his feet,
Each trial, each bitter loss,
And burdens of a hundred more;
He helps us bear the cross.
Consecrated by our Lord
With apostolic light,
Consecrated in his soul
He makes our darkness bright.
A loving radiance he sheds
That comes from God to man.
And we who walk in life-long night,
Can see as others can.
Although his tender, loving face
From us is shut apart,
We see the gracious wisdom
Of his understanding heart.
We feel a peace within his soul
And know a peace our own.
We hear his silent prayer that tells
We do not walk alone.
His faith in us will give us strength,
As unseen paths we trod;
Our souls uplifted by a man,
In partnership with God.

I stood at President Smith's bedside in his home and held his hand when he died at 7:27 P.M. on April 4, 1951. It was his eighty-first birthday. His tombstone is a flat granite marker that covers the entire grave in the Salt Lake Cemetery. Among other things, his epitaph reads: "He understood and disseminated the teachings of Christ, and was uncommonly successful in putting them into practice. He was kindly, patient, wise, tolerant and understanding.

He went about doing good. We are all our Father's children."

I spent many Christmases with President George Albert Smith. The cherished memories of that wonderful period in my life have helped me understand and appreciate more than words can tell the love of our Lord and Savior, Jesus Christ, the beautiful story of his lowly birth in a manger, and the good and humble men whom He has chosen to direct his kingdom here upon the earth.

Because of the living examples I have witnessed as I have served with seven Presidents of the Church during the last fifty years, I believe that the true meaning of Christmas is to love the Lord, love your neighbor, and *go about doing good!*

THE CHRISTMAS I REMEMBER MOST

D. Arthur Haycock

Fifty-seven years ago, President Harold B. Lee was my high school seminary teacher. During the summer months, he went door-to-door selling encyclopedias. On April 10, 1941, he was ordained an apostle by President Heber J. Grant. On February 10, 1947, he ordained me a bishop in the Pioneer Stake, where he lived at the time. On June 4, 1954, President Lee spoke at the farewell for our family when I was called to preside over the Hawaii Mission. On July 7, 1972, he was sustained as the eleventh President of The Church of Jesus Christ of Latter-day Saints, following which he asked me to be his personal secretary.

As President Lee's secretary, I was blessed to be with him on a daily basis, and I traveled the world with him.

The latter part of December 1973 I accompanied President Lee to New York City. The weather was bitter cold and his schedule was heavy. We returned home on December 23, somewhat weary from the long trip. The next day, Christmas Eve, he did not come to the office, but he asked me to bring the mail to his home. He always went out

Christmas Eve to deliver candy and flowers to his friends and neighbors, and particularly the widows of General Authorities. I could see he was tired, so I volunteered to deliver the gifts for him, and he was only too glad to have me do it.

President Lee spent Christmas Day with his daughter, Helen Goates, and family, and also visited the graves of his first wife, Fern, and their daughter, Maurine. The day after Christmas the president didn't come to the office, but again he asked me to bring his mail to him, which I did around one o'clock in the afternoon. He hadn't rested well during the night, so when the doctor came to check him, he suggested that, inasmuch as it was the holiday season, it might be a good time for the President to have his annual check-up.

I took President and Sister Lee up to LDS Hospital at 3:00 P.M. We entered quietly through a back door and went directly to room number 819. Soon after his arrival, the President underwent the usual routine exams, which were, of course, somewhat tiring. He hadn't eaten all day, but early in the evening he

41

had a nice supper and then stretched out for a rest. Sister Lee needed to return home for a while to check on a few things, so I said I would remain in the room with the President until she returned.

I sat by the bed and read the paper while also keeping an eye on the President. About 8:00 P.M. he suddenly turned toward me and sat up in bed. As I stood there with my hand on his shoulder, he spoke briefly to me, and then his face turned ashen and he began to perspire profusely. He did not respond when I talked to him; he was not concentrating on me, and his eyes were not focused. I laid him back on the bed and stepped to the door and called a nurse, who was just a few feet away. She came in with a wheelchair and indicated that if he was now awake she would take him for a scheduled X-ray.

The nurse didn't seem overly concerned, but I still didn't like the way the President looked, so I stepped to the door and called a doctor who was nearby. All of this transpired within thirty seconds. As I held the door and stood back to let the doctor enter, he took one look at the President and exclaimed, "Cardiac arrest—sound the alarm."

The doctor rushed over to the bed and began to massage the President's chest; at the same time the nurse called the operator, and soon the loudspeaker was repeating: "Dr. C. Arrest—819, Dr. C. Arrest—819." In a moment, doctors and nurses came running from every direction bringing special equipment with them.

I stayed in the room for a while, but I was no help, so I paced up and down the hall. In the meantime I called Sister Lee, and then President Tanner, who was in Arizona for the holidays, and also President Romney. As time wore on, I became convinced that unless the Lord worked a miracle, President Lee wasn't going to live. (The doctor later told me that the President had died the moment he spoke to me.)

It then occurred to me that the next President of the Church should be at the hospital, so I called President Spencer W. Kimball, President of the Quorum of the Twelve. President Kimball answered in his usual cheerful manner, asking, "Well, Arthur, how are you tonight?" I replied, "I'm not very well. I am at the hospital. President Lee is very sick, and I think you should come at once." He said, "I'll be right there." Just as I hung up, President Romney, second counselor to President Lee, came through the door.

It was on this sad occasion, the day after Christmas, one that I will never forget, that I learned a great lesson in priesthood and Church government. It was for me a sobering experience. As soon as Elder Kimball, President of the Quorum of the Twelve, arrived, he turned to President Romney of the First Presidency and asked, "President Romney, what would you like me to do?" He replied, "I think all we can do just now is pray and wait."

It wasn't long thereafter that the doctor came to the room where Sister Lee and the Brethren were waiting and said, "I am sorry. We did all we could and worked with him for more than an hour. He's gone!"

The moment a President of the Church dies, the First Presidency is dissolved and the counselors return to the Quorum of the Twelve in the order of their seniority. As soon as the doctor had finished speaking, President Romney turned to President Kimball and said, "President Kimball, what would you like me to do?" The mantle of the Presidency had changed that quickly and that quietly. There was no question in anyone's mind as to who would be President Lee's successor.

The Lord had set the pattern—it would be a man whom the Lord had chosen thirty years before as an apostle and special witness of his Son, Jesus Christ, Spencer Woolley Kimball, the senior apostle and president of the Quorum of the Twelve. President Kimball was sustained as the President of the Church on December 30, 1973. I served as his personal secretary until his death on November 5, 1985.

Christmas 1973 was a sad but memorable time in my life, but a time that has been forever engraved upon my mind. "When one door closes, another opens."

A SMITH FAMILY CHRISTMAS

Amelia Smith McConkie

On the day before Christmas, my sister Julina sat me on the kitchen table while she scrubbed the floor. Mama's house was always spotless, and she insisted it be particularly so for the holidays. It was a good-sized kitchen, so it took a while to scour; but I was happy as Julina regaled me with stories of Santa while she worked. Santa lived at the icy North Pole with his merry wife, his tireless, industrious elves, and his reindeer who magically transported him through the air.

Santa's sleigh paused on each housetop, and down the chimney he came to deliver just the right gift to each sleeping child. If a child had been good, Julina told me, Santa would leave something wonderful indeed; but if not, well then, Santa had a reward for that, too. This was always the case, Julina said solemnly, and Santa knew who had behaved and who had not.

As for me, she added mysteriously, she knew personally that Santa had something in his pack—something black, shiny, and pretty. I would be happy, she promised, because I had been good. "Tell me, tell me!" I begged, but I was not to have another word.

I was one of eleven rambunctious children waiting so impatiently for Christmas every year. I was named Amelia after my maternal grandmother, and took my place near the middle of the family. Before me were Josephine, Julina, Naomi, Emily, Lois, and Joseph. After me came my younger brothers, Lewis, Reynolds, Douglas, and Milton.

Our adored papa was Joseph Fielding Smith, the most tenderhearted father in all the world. Our mama was Ethel Georgina Reynolds, who kept our spirited crew in order. When we misbehaved, our papa would put his hands on our shoulders and say, "I wish my kiddies would be good." Papa's words went straight into our hearts. We hoped never to disappoint him. When we misbehaved, our mama rapped us quickly on the head with her thimble, which produced a similar effect.

The closer Christmas approached, the more saintly we endeavored to be, but our deportment was not to be overcome by our curiosity. For weeks Papa car-

44

ried packages, all sizes and shapes, into his library when he thought we were not watching, and then he carefully locked the door. Who were these bundles for, and what was in them? Lois and Joseph were just tall enough to stand on a chair, look over the transom, and describe for the rest of us what they saw. Lois told Joseph to boost her up to the open transom. "I can slip right through this gap," she said, "drop to the floor, and unlock the door," which she did.

Papa's library was a treasury containing illustrated encyclopedias, the *Book of Knowledge*, Charles Dickens's complete works, bound copies of *National Geographic* from the first issue, copies of the *Saturday Evening Post* with their wonderful covers, *Liberty* magazines, and countless other treasures. It was here that Papa kept the Nauvoo Legion sword belonging to Hyrum Smith, and the intriguing memorabilia of his father, Joseph F. Smith, including his left-handed golf sticks.

Our greatest interest in Papa's library was his set of Chatterboxes. As a boy, Papa received one Chatterbox and an orange each Christmas. The Chatterbox was a book about the size of a *Book of Knowledge*, and each volume was devoted to a different subject such as travel, science, adventure, fairy tales, or poetry. They were exquisitely illustrated. Papa had kept every volume and took very good care of them, as he did with everything he had, and as he wished we would do with our gifts and belongings.

Once we were in Papa's library, we could conjecture to our heart's content, but we had to be careful. Papa knew if so much as a string was out of place. He kept his rolltop desk locked so we couldn't get into the hardtack, or the chocolates, or the nuts. We would never chance touching the oranges or apples in the cases on the floor, because he would know for sure we had been there.

Evenings we younger children were herded to bed with solemn warnings. "Now then," Mama would intone to the rhythm of her forefinger, "you children are not to come downstairs until morning, do you hear?" Then Mama, Josephine, and Julina would secret themselves in the dining room, stitching away on the shirts, trousers, dresses, nighties, and slips that would appear on Christmas morning. Even our beautiful and intricate doll clothes were manufactured there.

"What are you doing downstairs?" I cried. "I want to come down there." My tears were not subdued by Mama's reassurances from the bottom of the stairs. I slept with Josephine, and the room was very lonely without her there. "There are spooks up here," I hollered. I was then allowed down and into the sewing circle, but everything was covered with sheets, and nothing was to be learned from their conversation. How could things be so very dull in there? Before long I was fast asleep, carted upstairs, and tucked in bed completely unaware.

I would have slept soundly, too, had

not Joseph, Lois, Emily, and Naomi taken it into their heads to jump on the beds of the younger children and yell, "It's Christmas! It's Christmas! Santa has already come!"

"If you children do not behave," Mama called, "you will get exactly what you deserve," and once again we trundled off to bed.

A week or so before Christmas, Papa would provide the opportunity for us to do something nice for one another. Coming home from the office with a wallet of crisp dollar bills, he proceeded through the house calling each child and dispensing this bounty according to age. We were close enough to town to walk easily to Woolworth's or one of the other stores on Main Street where we could purchase spectacular gifts for very little money and no tax.

In those days Emily thought herself cursed. She had beautiful red hair that she wove into long braids and then wrapped around her head. But her hair was not pretty to her. "No one," she wept pathetically, "will ever want to marry a redheaded girl with freckles." I wanted something nice for Emily. I rejected one possibility after another until I found Woolworth's diamond rings. I knew they were real; furthermore, they only cost ten cents. "This is exactly what I should get Emily," I thought. "How else will she ever get one?" That purchase made me very happy.

On Christmas Eve, Papa assembled us all in the parlor. The house was scrubbed and polished and so were we.

Mama played our favorite carols on the piano. She had taught piano, but now, encumbered by family cares, she seldom had time to touch the keys. Our papa told us the Christmas story, his words rising and falling in rich cadence, alive with his testimony. Finally, Papa brought out his good, woolen knee-high socks. These were to hang by the fireplace. These stockings could hold a great deal of candy, popcorn, and nuts. They were, we thought, perfectly suited to their purpose.

Papa wondered if Santa really would come. We assured him that Santa would be there. Well, off to bed then," Papa told us, "and do not come downstairs before 5:00 A.M." We went, reminding both Papa and Mama how good we had been.

What happened next has become a matter of record in the unofficial Smith family history. I shall tell it to you as we read it around the fireplace each Christmas Eve, and as chronicled by my nine-year-old granddaughter, Mary Fielding:

The Christmas Hideaway
The closer it got to Christmas, the more secrets there were. The younger children stayed on their beds imagining, and the oldest girls got to stay up all night sewing with Mama and making presents. Every night for the week before Christmas, Naomi, Emily, Lois, and Joseph sneaked into the littlest children's rooms and pounced on their beds, yelling, "Wake up, wake up,

Santa Claus has been here!" Up jumped the little kids and ran downstairs, but there was no Santa Claus and no Christmas.

Finally Papa set up tables in the living room. Mama covered every table with a sheet that hung to the floor. All of the children chose a spot where Santa would leave their things, and everyone went to bed. They had sugarplums in their heads, but Naomi and Emily and Lois and Joseph waited for all the lights to go out. They tiptoed downstairs to wait for Santa. Papa heard a noise. He went downstairs. Naomi and Emily and Lois and Joseph were in trouble. They scrambled around and got under the tables with the big tablecloths.

Papa came into the room and took a book off the shelf and sat down and read and read for hours. Very early in the morning, Papa went to bed and Santa still had not been there. Naomi and Emily and Lois and Joseph tiptoed upstairs and went to bed. At last it was morning and Santa Claus had come. Amelia and Lewis and Douglas and

baby Milton jumped on everyone's beds.

"Get up, get up," they said. "It's Christmas and Santa has been here!" But Naomi and Emily and Lois and Joseph were too tired to care. (Mary Fielding Adams.)

What rascals! But justice was tempered with mercy. Papa lined us all up, and into the Christmas parlor we went. The room was magnificent with Mama's handiwork hanging all about the molding, and all the gifts piled on the tables, and the red-and-green sugar candy animals hanging on the tree. Each childish heart was filled with joy. There in my spot was a new doll with a head that rotated expressions from happy to sad to sleeping, books and games, and the wonderful, shiny, black patent leather shoes I had always wanted, just as Julina had hinted.

Everything remained as it was until New Year's Day, when it was all put away, the tree carried out, and the house again put to rights. And we could hardly wait for Christmas to come once again.

CHRISTMAS WHEN
THE CUPBOARD WAS BARE

Victor and Lois Cline

This was the Christmas when four of our nine children were serving on missions at the same time. Our identical twin sons, Chris and Rick, were first called to serve in Ecuador and Peru. Then six months later our oldest daughter, Janice, was called to Taiwan. And finally Robyn left for the Toronto, Canada, area.

At the following April Conference it was announced that there were 30,004 missionaries serving around the world. And, at least in our family, we knew who those four were. At a later stake conference, our stake president, Merlin Lybbert, mentioned the same statistic and summarized that those "four" must be from the Cline family.

I was supporting eleven people on a professor's salary plus doing a little consulting on the side. It seemed that no matter how much money came in each month, we were spending still more. Our policy on cars was to run them until they dropped, then run them some more. Most of our children learned to drive on our dusty brown

Toyota. But each left a special mark of distinction on that old car—a dented fender here, or a slightly caved-in bumper there. We hesitated to do much body repair work because we knew there was a high probability of still more crunches coming later, as other children reached their sixteenth birthdays.

I hated to park that car in front of our home on the street where we lived. I'm sure our neighbors cringed every time they drove by. But the money for the needed repairs just wasn't there.

With four missionaries in the field, we approached Christmas a little differently that year than we had in the past. Some previous Christmases at our home had found Santa leaving an endless array of gifts and goodies under the Christmas tree for our eleven family members. No matter how we had sworn to be more frugal and prudent in our gift-giving, emotion had always overridden prudence and we had typically kept adding more gifts to the pile as

Christmas Day approached.

We didn't want anybody to get overlooked or shorted.

But this Christmas was different. Our resources were meager; the cupboard was nearly bare.

As my wife, Lois, and I counseled together, we decided to handle Christmas this year somewhat differently than before. There would be only one modest gift for each family member, and we decided to especially emphasize the spiritual significance of the Savior's life and birth.

The commercial aspect would be almost entirely missing. No fighting the crowds at the malls or worrying if some present was too expensive for one child, which might make another youngster jealous for not getting something of equal value.

As we explained our tight financial circumstances to our children and outlined our plans for Christmas, we squirmed a little. It was hard to imagine what Christmas morning would look like with very little in the way of gifts and bounties around the tree. But we knew there was no other choice. So much of our resources were going to support our missionaries that something had to give.

On the other hand, however, we felt a quiet joy in being able to serve our Father in Heaven through our children. It was a family effort that united us.

Our children all took the news about the coming Christmas in easy stride. They caught the spirit of what we were doing, and each in their own way became excited about being creative in their gift-making and gift-giving. Each took seriously the challenge to create something that wouldn't come from the store but would be unique and lovely. We each drew names to see who would give a gift to whom. And that was to be kept secret until Christmas morning.

So for some weeks each child furtively worked on a secret project (as Lois and I did also), making sure that no one could tell what they were making. When the gifts were completed they were wrapped and placed under the tree. It then became a guessing game to figure out what each funny-shaped object was. Sometimes one of the children would touch or lift or shake a gift to figure out what it was — only to be loudly and severely chastened by its creator.

A few days before Christmas, at a family home evening, we asked family members to write a "dialogue" expressing their thoughts on the subject, "What the Savior means to me." All ages were asked to participate. For about ten minutes we all silently wrote our reflections and feelings about this topic.

Sometimes it is easier to write about very tender feelings than it is to express them outloud in a group. When everyone was finished, we asked if anyone would care to share with the family his or her "dialogue." With some hesitancy at first, one and then another and then another read aloud to the rest of us what they had written.

This proved to be one of the most moving spiritual experiences our family had ever participated in. By the time everyone was finished, there wasn't a dry eye in the room. Somehow this exercise had provided an unrestrained way for there to be a straight-from-the-heart expression of faith that could be shared with the whole family. This tender experience reminded each of us of the importance of the Savior in our lives and set the stage for our Christmas celebration.

Finally Christmas morning arrived. While there were not the huge stacks of presents common to previous years, everything under the tree had been thoughtfully and carefully crafted by the hands and hearts of each family member. So there was an extra special interest and anticipation to see and hear the squeals of surprise and reactions as we opened our gift packages. It was quite different from the Christmas mornings in previous years when we opened the store-bought gifts. The spirit of our Father in Heaven was with us in abundance.

Christmas that year was like no other Christmas we had ever experienced in our family. The joy was overflowing.

We each felt that our cup was more than filled.

Surprisingly, in the succeeding months there was always money enough to pay our bills, eat nutritious meals, handle music lessons, and take care of the essentials. I'm not sure how we did it. And there were occasional contributions to the children's mission fund from anonymous others. We were truly blessed.

The day finally came when all of our children who'd been serving in distant lands returned home. Three arrived within a day or two of each other. What a joyous reunion!

And in following years, as our finances became more balanced, we reverted to the customary ways of celebrating Christmas, with most everything being purchased in stores. But it has never been the same. We have never quite recaptured the wonderful experience of Christmas as that year when we had four missionaries serving—when the cupboard was bare—and when we chose to honor the Savior's birthday in a more simple, humble, spiritual way.

That is a Christmas we'll always remember.

GIFT FROM THE HEART

Sharlene Wells Hawkes

Every December when we lived in Argentina, my two sisters and I counted the days until school broke for the summer and Christmas vacation—which are one and the same in that part of the world. On December 16 finals were over, and we would rush home, pack the Suburban, and embark on our annual Christmas journey to Bariloche, in the southern Andes of Argentina.

Bariloche! Just the name conjures for me more vivid Yuletide memories than a picture of a robust Santa on a sleigh. It was a magical dream-place for all of us: a Swiss-type village with cobble-stone streets and bright, red-shuttered windows nestled in the lap of thickly forested mountains, on the edge of Na-huel Huapi, a mirror-smooth, blue-as-Paul-Newman's-eyes lake.

The yearly tradition originated with my father's zone conference scheduling. He was to tour the Bahia Blanca Mission our first December after we had moved to Buenos Aires in 1977. Because he had served near Bariloche as a missionary, Dad knew all of us would love to accompany him and Mom on this tour. Church meetings and plea-sure combined, it seemed the most practical way to be together for more than the usual three days at a time.

That first Christmas stands out in my mind the clearest, probably because the sheer impact of discovering such a "secret" (most people outside Argentina have never heard of it) was stunning. Our hotel was equally inspiring: Built upon a hill that overlooked Nahuel Hu-api on one side and a smaller, even bluer lake on the other, it had the look and homey feel of an Aspen ski lodge, yet the size and grandeur of Buck-ingham Palace.

Instead of typical presents, we gave each other "coupons"—our version of the "gift-from-the-heart" idea. My sister Elayne presented me with a coupon worth five typing jobs (as I often had papers due for school, this was a much-welcomed gift), and I gave my father a coupon good for ten back rubs. Janet offered to help Mom with cooking whenever she needed her, and Mom's present to me was a sewing lesson once a week (all coupons good for six months).

We exchanged the coupons in our

little suite of adjoining rooms with hard oak floors and multipaned, windowed views of pine-crested peaks. Janet, Elayne, and I had tiptoed past the bathroom to our parents' room at 6:30 A.M., more anxious to open up our coupon-presents than we had been the year before to see what Santa had brought.

Somehow, the feeling of Christmas had changed.

I recorded the following in my journal: "Everyone got one of their socks and we hung them by the fireplace, and then everyone put their coupons in everyone's sock. First we read some really neat Christmas stories about the birth of Christ. It made me glad that we were giving coupons this year; it seemed like more a kind of Christmas that He would want."

Instead of parties, we went horseback riding by the lake on a muggy Christmas Eve, and Christmas morning (after giving the coupons) we attended a zone conference where Dad instructed the missionaries, and my sisters and I sang Christmas hymns in trio, Mom accompanying on the piano.

After the conference, for Christmas dinner, we had pasta and garlic bread at a small Italian restaurant in the middle of the village—the reason being, in part, that we had spontaneously added about twenty new members to our family that morning, and turkey in Argentina is too expensive for a missionary's budget. The look on the proprietor's face when he saw all twenty-five of us come in (most were fair-haired *gringos*) was priceless.

We stayed in Bariloche another day, and then it was off across the Andes to southern Chile for more missionary and member meetings.

For three years we spent Christmas in Bariloche. Our last year we held a "Bariloche Poem Contest" on the trip back, and the winning poem has been a family classic since:

Christmas Day in Bariloche
Is one we'll never forget;
With snow on the mountains,
Horses and flowers,
And lakes that'll get you wet.
(If you fall in)

The days are peaceful,
The nights full of rest,
The people friendly and nice.
But beware in the winter,
When there's snow all around,
That you don't slip on the ice.

The days are warm,
With a nice cool breeze,

The lake smooth as a mirror.
But be careful of the bees
That hide in the bushes—
They'll sting you if you get any nearer.

Well, our stay at the
Llao-Llao Hotel was real neat;
Everything was dandy.
After riding horses,
We went into town,
And bought some chocolate candy.

And so we left on Tuesday morn—
We were headed for the border.
We met some soldiers on the way,
Their tanks were all in order.

But the thing we'll most remember
Is a feeling you can't put in words;
When you give from the heart
You know it's a start
And the family's all happy as birds!

Like I said,
We'll never forget
This beautiful trip down here.
With birds and bees
And big pine trees
And heaven that seemed so near.

CHRISTMAS ALONE

Marilyn Arnold

In a sense Christmas has not been one holiday for me, but many holidays. As I have changed, and my circumstances have changed, the season has altered considerably, although its signs and symbols have remained quite constant. Ever since I can remember, there has been the rather odd but happy combination of festivity and worship. There have been children on Santa's knee and children solemn in over-sized bathrobes next to a doll in a makeshift manger. There have always been red and green baubles and streamers, bells, holly, candy canes, stockings, and the second chapter of Luke recited to the strains of "Silent night, holy night." There have always been gifts extraordinary in their bright wrappings under a lighted tree, reduced to the ordinary when stripped of their mystery.

When I was a child, nearly everything associated with Christmas became a precious ritual, from the placing of the same ornament (the only decoration my parents could afford in the jobless days of their first Christmas together) at the top of the tree to the waffle supper that followed the hanging of the stockings on Christmas Eve. Then, there was the piling into the thick quilted bedcovers with whistles, horns, and other clanging things to await the six o'clock yell from my brothers: "Merry Christmas! Turn up the stoker!"

The house rule strictly forbade children to arise until the furnace, fed by a stoker my father filled with coal every morning and evening, had warmed the house. We gathered in eager anticipation before the closed door that separated kitchen from living room—I having spent the night with hands clamped over my ears, praying for sleep that would make morning come more quickly. At some unspoken signal, Father opened the door and we burst into a room transformed. I raced to the big chair where my gifts were invariably placed.

There was not much money in those days, and our gifts were modest by any standards, but to us they were a dream come true. One year a neighbor made a wooden sled with "Neddie" painted on it for my younger brother. Another year my old tricycle sat shining in a new coat of orange paint for him, and a new

54

red scooter greeted me. Still another year there was a very adult pocket watch and chain for one of the boys. Every year, in the seat of honor, there was a new teddy bear for me, to replace what was left of last year's one-eyed, ragged-eared lump of matted fur. And always, there was at least one book apiece from our favorite series: for the boys, *Little Woodsman of the North* or *Little Philip of Wales*; for me, *Little Ann of Canada* or *Little Greta of Denmark*. Later there were books like *A Girl of the Limberlost*, a title that still sounds mysterious and wonderful—"Limberlost."

In my teen years, I was the spirit of Christmas personified—loving the season with a joyous passion that I now view with nothing short of amazement. I started playing Christmas carols in November, and didn't let up until January. I wrapped gifts weeks in advance and delighted in seeing them spill out from under the tree. I loved decorating cookies and visiting relatives, especially Myrene, who made wonderful home-dipped chocolates. There was an unspoken agreement among my brothers and me that we spent Christmas Eve at home—no dates, no parties, just family singing and reading together and keeping alive the beloved rituals of our childhood.

And then one day the shine was gone. Reluctant to admit it, even to myself, I kept up the act for years, sometimes driving many long miles through terrifying storms in order to be "home for Christmas." As I grew older, the season seemed to bring less peace and joy than a heightened sense of pain and loss. Surrounded by celebration, the person without spouse or children perhaps becomes more acutely aware than at other times of a cavern somewhere deep inside. Connections that ordinarily are strong and satisfying seem perilously thin and tentative. The feeling of aloneness grows more acute, even if one is not actually alone. Sensitized by the season, I became aware of a universal sorrow at Christmastime among others—those grieving for lost loved ones, those hungering for lost opportunities, those suffering from illness and pain, those yearning for a home.

This undercurrent of sorrow began to define Christmas for me, though I had some bright moments as I plowed dutifully through the seasonal observances. I began dreading the approach of the season, then struggling through it and feeling immense relief at the arrival of December 26. What a change this was from my childhood, when I physically hurt each Christmas night to hear my father launch into his annual rendition of "Dinner is done, night has come, worn and tired are they. Gun won't shoot, horn won't toot, blocks all lost but ten. But never fear, just wait one year, old Chris will come again. . . . " As he sang, I ached with the realization that it was over; and it was no consolation that in just one year, Christmas would return with all its splendor and gladness. I remember silently begging him not to sing that song because it was the world's saddest song to me. But he always sang it. To go from

55

dreading the day's passing to earnestly wishing it past was indeed a change.

Each succeeding year seemed more difficult than the last, and family gatherings, much as I love my brothers and their wives and children, more painful. They seemed so secure in their own separate family circles that the more they tried to draw me in, the more I felt excluded. I found myself wanting simply to slip away to some unknown place, the desert perhaps, at Christmastime. But that was never possible, because my parents and the others were counting on me.

Then about four years ago, and for the first time in my life, I found myself with no obligations at Christmastime. My parents flew to Australia to spend Christmas with one brother's family; my brother in Utah was involved with his children and their families, and they, thankfully, did not insist that I join them; and the women with whom I share a home had gone to visit family out of state. Instead of escaping, I stayed in my mountain home, isolated, adrift with snow, the nearest neighbor some distance away. I will never forget that Christmas Eve as I did battle with my soul, coming to terms at last with the prospect of hating Christmas for the rest of my life, or casting aside self-pity to join with others of God's children in glad celebration of the Savior's birth.

My home, set deep in a forest of trees, seemed especially empty that night, and I nearly succumbed to de-

spair. Then I got hold of myself, pulled out the piano bench, and began playing and singing Christmas carols. It was a choir of one, but since there was no congregation to take offense, the services went quite well. And then, finally, I turned for consolation to first sources. I read Nephi's sorrowful, urgent prayer as the faithful watched for the sign of the Savior's birth while the faithless taunted and threatened them. And I thought how he must have rejoiced when the Lord answered him, saying, "Lift up your head and be of good cheer; for behold, the time is at hand, and on this night shall the sign be given, and on the morrow come I into the world." (3 Nephi 1:13.) The reason for his coming, and the reason why Christmas means what it does to us, the Savior himself announced thirty-three years later in the dense stillness that followed broad destruction and mourning: "Behold, I have come unto the world to bring redemption unto the world, to save the world from sin." (3 Nephi 9:21.)

I remember feeling less lonely, though still a bit shaky, as I crawled into bed that night. But ever since, I have had the impression that I crossed a line in those hours that I will not have to cross again. Each succeeding Christmas, though scarcely a match for the joyous seasons of my youth, has confirmed the gloriousness of the Savior's announcement to the Nephites, and the value of many hearts acknowledging it together.

CHRISTMAS PRESENT AND CHRISTMAS PAST

Pat Edwards

It's delightful to visit grandchildren anytime and anywhere, and it is especially exciting to visit them at Christmastime.

One December I spent the first five days in New York City with my grandchildren, Andrea and Matthew Edwards. Andrea was eight years old, and Matthew was two. They were living in New York while their father completed his residency in orthopedic surgery.

New York City dresses up with Christmas lights and decorations. Buildings no longer resemble each other as they become Christmas ornaments for Manhattan. For instance, the Cartier building is wrapped in a red ribbon, giving it the appearance of a gigantic package.

One morning we visited the windows of Sak's Fifth Avenue. They were alive with animated characters from the C. S. Lewis novel *The Lion, the Witch and the Wardrobe.*

Someone whispered, "I understand that it cost the store $150,000.00 to do these decorations."

The speaker made the statement as though the cost could make the chimerical scene more beautiful and impressive. Those of us who feasted our eyes upon that wondrous sight were mesmerized. And perhaps we would have stayed longer looking at the windows, but the chill in the weather made us move on.

The block was long, and soon the Sak's windows were forgotten and reality set in. Not far from those fairy-tale windows stood a man who was blind, holding out his cup for charity. Just past him was a man who was selling pencils. He was on a skateboard. We learned that he had lost his legs in Vietnam. Another man was lying on the sidewalk. A bag at his side contained all of his earthly possessions. These people were just some of the one hundred thousand homeless people—one-third of them children under the age of four—living on the streets of Manhattan. The homeless crisis is something that we don't always like to think about—especially at Christmastime. But it was sobering to contemplate as we walked the streets.

That year I was overwhelmed with the contrasts of Christmas—the chimerical, the reality. Few people stopped to share quarters with those men. And as I held Matthew's hand, I suddenly wondered about man's love for man. Where was it—was it tinseled? I also couldn't help but recall the Christmas when I was five. That year, we had been homeless.

Three weeks before Christmas my parents and I went to my grandparents' house for supper. Although they lived just across the street from us, we bundled up in our warm coats, hats, mittens, and overshoes, because it was a cold evening—fifty degrees below zero.

We had been there about an hour when we heard someone yell, "Fire, fire!" Then there was a pounding on my grandparents' door.

Our neighbor, Mr. Burney, yelled, "Fire, the Covey's home is on fire! Is Patti Lou here?"

"Yes, she is here," someone called back to him.

My parents ran out into the cold night and raced toward our home. It was a blazing inferno. Our dog, Spark Plug, was in the house. Mother kicked in a window to let him out. In the process she cut an artery in her leg, an injury that hospitalized her for a week.

Someone had called the fire department, and soon the fire truck was there. But it was useless, because the water was frozen inside the hose. Our neighbors and other people from our town formed a bucket brigade to fight the flames.

Within forty-five minutes our home burned to the ground. The three of us were homeless and destitute. The flames had taken everything. Our only possessions were the clothes we had on our backs and our dog.

Fortunately for us, we were able to move in with my grandparents, and that helped. But it was still a difficult period for all of us, especially my father and mother.

One of the difficult things they had to do was to tell me that Santa Claus wouldn't be able to visit us. This year, they explained, it was our turn to let him visit other children.

I can't remember much about what happened those next few weeks before Christmas. I do, however, recall having mother come home from the hospital, and the children's party that was held in the community hall.

The week before Christmas, Santa Claus would visit the community hall in Big Piney. He would have popcorn balls and bags of candy that he passed out to all of the children. That year, my bag of candy was especially important to me, because I felt that was going to be my only gift from him.

After he gave it to me, I ran and gave it to my mother with the admonition, "Keep this for me, and I will put it under the Christmas tree." I was excited about the candy because it would be a present from Santa and would satisfy my sweet tooth.

Like all children, I didn't sleep much Christmas Eve. Christmas has a magic that can make children sleepless.

The next morning when I walked into the living room where my grandparents' Christmas tree was, I saw a Shirley Temple doll. Then I saw other presents that were meant for a five-year-old child.

"Santa did come!" I exclaimed with excitement.

As I turned to my parents, I saw that they too had a look of surprise on their faces. And the tears in their eyes expressed their joy that Santa hadn't forgotten us.

We later learned that Santa had many helpers that year. The people in Big Piney opened up their hearts and their purses to make our Christmas happy.

We were nine months without a home. But we lived in a small town where people cared about each other. For me, that year man's love for man kept the tinsel out of Christmas.

As the years have passed, that Christmas has become more significant to me—not because of the presents we received, but because of the service rendered to us.

And isn't that what Christmas is about—service? The service given to us by Christ our Savior, and in return the service that we can render to our fellowmen.

As I held Andrea's and Matthew's hands that day as we walked the streets of Manhattan, I thought of my Christmas as a five-year-old girl and cherished the memory. It is a time I shall never forget.

CHRISTMASES TO REMEMBER

JoAnn Ottley

Contribute to a book of Christmas memories and experiences? What a flood of emotions and remembrances that invitation brings, and what an adventure in personal enlightenment as I realize the impossibility of trying to separate Christmas and music. The two are inextricably woven together as far back as my memory can reach. That's not so unusual, of course. Hardly anyone can remember a Christmas without music. They go together. The difference for a musician, and perhaps especially a singer, is that the music (and the music making) *is* Christmas.

As I reach back, I am surprised at the varied levels of impact those memories have as they present themselves. How can I sort them out in any fashion that would be of value to any reader? Perhaps it would be expected for me to concentrate on the unusual musical and professional experiences I've had at Christmastime—all those for which I got dressed up, got the applause, and got paid. Yet, as I think about the meaning of Christmas and the invitation to recall the holidays that stand out most in my mind, I realize that the

memories worth writing about aren't the fancy ones.

By saying that, I don't mean to negate or downplay the wonderful and rich experiences I've had, especially in all those performances of Handel's *Messiah* with fine orchestras, conductors, and singers around the country. How fortunate can one person be, to sit among the master musicians, surrounded by those magnificent sounds, and offer up a part in that great work? It is thrilling to take part in special Christmas celebrations, sometimes with or for celebrities, and perform some of the world's finest music. It must certainly be one of heaven's sweetest blessings to be a singer. I am fortunate, and I know it.

Nevertheless, I somehow find it surprising to reflect back on all those big performances and become aware of what stands out. One of those moments occurred a few years ago as I sat on the stage of Salt Lake City's Symphony Hall. It was a "sing-in" performance with the Utah Symphony Chorale and members of the Utah Symphony.

At the "sing-in," the "choir" was composed of the two thousand or so members of the audience, some of whom have at sometime or other sung the *Messiah,* some who sing only at Christmastime, and some who can scarcely find the notes when they do sing. One might expect that, on the basis of using a less-than-memorable choir in a largely unrehearsed performance, this would have been a precarious event at best. But there, a few feet in front of my front-stage soloist seat, stood a father and his young daughter, singing their hearts out on "For unto Us a Child Is Born," reading from a *Messiah* score that must have been a hundred years old. I don't know why, but it brought a tear then, and still does. And I remember the rush of emotion as I saw the sea of faces and felt the impact of their combined voices rolling over and through me as they sang "and the Lord has laid on Him the iniquity of us all." Suddenly I knew more deeply than ever the magnitude of the ransom.

I also think back to the time when I was invited to sing for the First Presidency's Christmas devotional. It was in the days when the devotional was held at the Church Administration Building for all who worked there — General Authorities, secretaries, everyone. I faced the audience as I sang, and by doing so had to stand directly in front of President David O. McKay, with my back to him. As I finished my last notes, I felt his hand slip into mine from behind. It was a kind of private thank you, a moment to remember.

Then there are the Christmas memories that come not from the fancy affairs, but from the simpler, deeper times. Songs of comfort performed at Christmastime funerals have burned their place in my memories, as have programs at rest homes. Only last Christmas, for example, as one of the volunteers at a health-care center in Salt Lake City wheeled her aged patient back to her room following my singing a few songs for them, the patient said to the volunteer, "I never heard a voice like that. Was it an angel?"

No, it wasn't. Not by any means. But I'd like to think that, until we are privileged to hear and, I hope, sing in the heavenly choirs, those of us who sing at Christmastime are doing our part to help them with a little of their work.

AN IDAHO CHRISTMAS
IN THE MID-1930S

Davis Bitton

When I was a child we lived in Black-foot, Idaho, which then had a population of less than five thousand. My father worked in a men's clothing store and eventually became one of the partners. But the country was not far away. Uncle R. A. and Aunt Anna (Davis) Carlson lived on a farm east of town, and five miles to the west, in Riverside, was the farm of my grandparents, John and Althea (Bingham) Bitton.

Winter was unusually cold the year I am remembering—forty below, not counting the chill factor. There was snow on the ground.

During the Christmas season we—Dad, Mother, my younger brother John Boyd, and I—drove out to visit my grandparents. There was electricity there. Sometimes they huddled around a radio to listen to programs. But in many ways Grandpa's farm seemed to be from pioneer times. The fields were cared for by horse-drawn plows and harrows and cultivators. Cows were milked by hand. It was a treat to take a glass from the kitchen and have

Grandpa fill it partially with fresh, warm, foamy milk. There was an outdoor privy—quite an adventure for those unused to this approach to life's necessities. Water was pumped by hand from a well, provided in troughs for the animals, and as needed brought by bucket, icy cold, into the house.

Although the house was large enough, it was in the kitchen that the family lived. Heating the other rooms was just too difficult in the days before central heating. A large, black kitchen range provided warmth, cooked the meals, and even contained hot water in a "reservoir" on one side. I still remember the smell of plum pudding as Grandma prepared it during that Christmas season.

When we returned to our home in town, we had a few more conveniences. But it was not a good year. Depression conditions still prevailed. Dad was fortunate to have a job, but more than once we heard, "Santa Claus is poor this year."

So we children didn't expect much.

There was a tree, and on Christmas Eve stockings were hung out. Mother read to us "The Other Wise Man" by Henry Van Dyke (a tradition she kept up for many years). But as we went to bed, we anticipated a skimpy Christmas morning.

The next day, to our delight, we found under the tree wondrous things. There were stick horses—broomsticks with stuffed heads made of oilcloth, bridles, and reins. There were cowboy suits—colorful shirts, neckerchiefs, hats, chaps, and little wooden guns. That was not all. There were desks for each of us. The tops lifted up, and inside were pencils, crayons, and stacks of paper.

It had all been done by the loving hands of a father and mother who, using what they could obtain, created a magical Christmas for two small boys. Some years later I came across Edna St. Vincent Millay's evocative poem "The Harp Weaver" and thought of my mother.

One other glimpse comes from that year. When we went to church in the old Blackfoot Second Ward, the choir put on a special Christmas cantata. Dad was the choir leader. Wide-eyed at the poinsettias placed in front of the chapel, noticing the excitement of performers who had been preparing for this night, then listening to the rich sounds of the organ and a choir singing of Jesus Christ, a small boy could even then realize, at least in part, that there was more to Christmas than just receiving gifts.

Mother presented a reading entitled "A Candle in the Forest." She had learned how to do these readings in her high school elocution class. The story was about a poor family that loved each other and a rich family next door where there was jealousy and hate. The small boy from the rich family was invited over to visit the poor family—a small girl and her loving parents. They could not afford turkey and the trimmings but did have a beefsteak pie. "The onions will be silver, and the carrots will be gold," said the small girl's mother. There was love in the simple home and magic and the true spirit of Christmas.

All of this was more than fifty years ago. To those who have grown up in the post-World War II period, who never remember a time without television, it must seem hard to imagine.

Thanks for the memories, for the times when onions were silver and carrots were gold.

THE GIFTS AND THE GIVER

Marilynne Linford

6:30 A.M., Christmas 1953

If there were ever perfect Christmases, they were the ones in the C. M. Todd home. As the oldest child, I should know—I'd been there the longest. I had four sisters and no brothers! We felt unique and blessed because there were no brothers. The only boys my sisters and I were acquainted with were the boys at school and a couple of boy cousins. That was sufficient evidence, as far as I was concerned, to know without doubt that only the most elect families had all girls. When I learned about the Creation, it made perfect sense that Eve was created last. "Last the best of all the game."

The excitement of Christmas filled the kitchen, and after the traditional delays of beds made, breakfast eaten, pictures taken in the line up—oldest to youngest—we were allowed to enter the living room to get our socks.

To our complete astonishment, we saw a smoke-puffing train circling the Christmas tree. Forgetting the bulging socks, we sat down to learn how to couple and uncouple cars, how to make the train go fast and slow, forward and backward. We saw that we could switch the train, or even part of the train, to a different track.

Later, as the gifts were opened, we found our requests for girlish things had been switched for more "attachments" for the train—plastic animals and people, a station, Lincoln Logs, blocks, and Tinker Toys. The question that Santa must have goofed lasted only a moment as we began to build bridges and buildings, load the cars, and experiment with the switching and coupling. We loved the choo-chooing sound and the sight of the gleaming headlight shining in the darkened room with whitish smoke trailing after. At top speed the train could almost catch the smoke from the last time around the track.

In the years that followed we received race car sets, other trains, a basketball standard, and three brothers. Maybe it was not so much our parents' wisdom in exposing girls to a boy's world as it was an act of faith. Perhaps they reasoned if they had all the toys, they would be "blessed" with boys.

Thanks for the gift of memory.

Christmas 1963

Everything was the same, but everything was different. The ring on my left hand was making it different. Next Christmas? Where would I be? How would my brothers and sisters have Christmas without me? Could I really leave the Todd family? Dad was passing out gifts. We were down to the last ones. I didn't need anything else. A present for me? I recognized the gift wrap. This was a book from Deseret Book. What book could be appropriate? I searched my mother's eyes for a clue. As I opened it, my eyes filled with tears. Yes. I could leave the family to make a new one. They would be fine without me. The gift, a leatherbound set of scriptures, signified it. These were my first scriptures and a treasure, but they were not the most significant part of that Christmas before my marriage. With this gift my parents stamped their approval on my choice. "It's right. Do it. You have our blessing." The book made it final, because there was a name imprinted in the lower righthand corner. The inscription read, "Marilynne Todd" (which I expected), then—"Linford."

Thanks for the gift of change.

A few weeks before Christmas 1981

"Dad."

"Yes, Matt."

"Dad, all us bigger kids have been talking and we don't want Christmas on Christmas."

"What?"

"We don't want Christmas on Christmas."

"Why? What do you mean?"

"Well, 'cause it's Sunday."

"And it won't seem like Christmas or Sunday if they come together," clarified eleven-year-old Michelle.

"How do you think it should work?" I asked.

"We will just get up and go to Church just like always," said ten-year-old Mike.

"Then we can have a nice home evening," continued eight-year-old Anne, as though she'd been told what to say.

"Read the Christmas story, sing Christmas songs . . . " continued Michelle.

"And go to bed early," contributed seven-year-old Elizabeth.

"See, Dad and Mom," Matt said, "then we can wake up early and it will be Christmas on Monday."

I was beginning to see. Our strict Sabbath rules were interfering with the children's idea of Christmas fun.

A few days later I found a poem written by Roxana F. Hase titled "Christmas on Sunday." The third stanza reads:

Oh, it was fun when I was a child
By the pot-bellied stove, my thoughts
    all beguiled
By the story of Jesus, so simple and
    true,
That he was God's baby without doubt
    I knew,
And I like it the best when his birthday
    came Sunday,

With one day for worship and a holiday
Monday.

That Christmas morning Richard and
I woke at seven o'clock with great anticipation. All was quiet. No one expected anything but a normal Sunday.
We went to each room and whispered,
"The Sabbath Santa left a gift." Soon
we were gathered around the tree.
There was one large gift (a box I had
covered inside and out with contact paper).

"Open it," I suggested.

They did so, and then poured the
contents—about thirty little gifts—onto
the carpet. There were journals, little
books about Old Testament prophets,
puzzles with Bible scenes, scripture
workbooks, a Noah-and-the-Ark wipe-
off tablecloth, an LDS game, and sta-
tionery and stamps.

With the rule that the "Sunday Box"
could only be used on Sundays, the
newness lasted for years. Yes, I like it
best when his birthday is Sunday, with
one day for worship and a holiday
Monday.

Thanks for the gift of ideas.

New Year's Eve 1987

The holiday season this year had
been different because of Sarah, my
niece. Her seven months of mortality
had challenged everyone who knew her
or heard of her. Her perfect little body,
angelic face, and expressionless eyes lay
unknowing day after day, month upon
month. The ever-so-long seconds between her erratic breaths and her bluish
color gave little hope of anything better.
The "why" would never be answered.
The, "How long will she stay?" was a
constant, foreboding thought. Her parents, brother, and sisters loved her,
played with her as with a doll, dressed
her, and looked deep into her eyes for
a glimpse of recognition.

During that Christmas many neighbors and friends had remembered Sarah's family in thoughtful ways. I
wanted to help, to ease the constant
stress.

In the afternoon on December 30,
Sarah was just too tired to take one
more breath. A peaceful transition to a
world of perfection was her gift. She
deserved to be free.

The next morning, New Year's Eve, I
prayed to know how to lift the sadness
in their hearts. Nothing came to mind.
So I went about my duties. I thought to
myself, "I'll call Rochelle as soon as I've
made the seven-layer dip and open-face
sandwiches" (our traditional New
Year's Eve menu). As I opened the refrigerator to begin, I felt a craving for
clam chowder. I went to each child and
asked if it was okay to break the tradition and have clam chowder. All but
two said that was fine. Those two
wanted chili. "All right," I thought.
"I'll make both."

It took more time than I'd planned,
but finally both were in the refrigerator.
The phone rang. It was Rochelle. I
asked how each of her children and
husband were dealing with the loss.

"And how are you doing?" I asked.

"Okay, but it's hard to gear up for

what's supposed to be a holiday."

"What do you usually do on New Year's Eve?"

"Just have our own family party, maybe watch a video and play games."

"What do you eat?"

"Always the same two things."

"What's that?" I asked.

"Chili and clam chowder."

Thanks for the gift of promptings.

Christmas Eve 1989

The ordeal began the day before Thanksgiving with a phone call. "We've been trying to reach you. There has been an accident at school. The paramedics are transporting Daniel to Primary Children's Hospital."

It was "just" a broken leg that cost Daniel, among other things, cancelling the trip to Idaho for Thanksgiving, five days in the hospital in a body cast, home for four days, back in the hospital in traction for ten days, in another body cast for four weeks, and two months of school missed. Nine-year-old Daniel spent his days on a fully reclining wheelchair and his nights in bed. It took several of us to move him. He couldn't go anywhere or do much for himself.

Christmas Eve, Sunday, it was Chris-

tine's turn to stay home with him while we went to Church. During the service, Richard whispered, "I'm going to ask the bishop if we can have the sacrament for Daniel. It's been five weeks since he's been to church. He's missed too much of everything."

That Sabbath Christmas Eve we had prayer, sang and read from Luke and 3 Nephi. Then we were privileged to have the ordinance of the sacrament. Matt, now a returned missionary, blessed the bread; Richard, the water. John, our deacon, passed them to us. We felt reverent, close, loved, and taken care of. We had all been inconvenienced because of Daniel's injury. One of us always had to be with him. We had to feed him, bathe him, and take care of every need. He needed someone to help with homework brought by his teacher, to play a game, or read to help fill the long days. But taking the sacrament on Christmas Eve in our home reminded us how tiny our sacrifices for a younger brother who could do little for himself really had been. Then we understood and felt, in a larger dimension, the love of an Older Brother who could have done everything for himself but chose not to. He epitomized the word *sacrifice*.

Thanks for the gift of thy Son.

HARMATTAN CHRISTMAS

Gloria W. Rytting

"He who eats and drinks of Africa will never be the same." —Anonymous

"Mom! Dad! Come quick! Something is happening outdoors in our compound!" yelled our nine-year-old son, shaking us from slumber. "Wake up! Wake up! It's Christmas!"

Rubbing our eyes, my husband and I threw on light robes and followed him outdoors into the cool West Africa air. Our ears picked up sounds of gongs, bells, and drums as we made out a cluster of burlap-clad masqueraders presenting a Christmas morning performance for our family. Onlookers clapped and swayed as youthful musicians shuffled back and forth, stomping up clouds of red dust that settled on harmattan lilies and bougainvillea in our garden and dislodged orange headed geckos (lizards) that darted for cover.

Their costumes, made of loosely woven burlap, completely covered their heads and bodies. Colorful raffia skirts were tied around waists and shoulders; straw-like headdresses poked up like rooster tails on their heads; and beads, shells, and bells adorned necks and

ankles. Sturdy leather oxfords seemed out of harmony with their costumes. I surmised from their size and accompanying entourage that our Christmas performers were children about the same age as Kent, our youngest. The noise and excitement heightened as our three older children and other neighbors joined us to watch the spectacle.

As the dancing, laughter, and celebration gained momentum, a neighbor whispered that the dancers would expect a "dash" or tip for their entertainment. As the benefit concert wound down, my husband gave each performer a few *kobos* (pennies) and thanked them for coming to bless us with their festive dancing. With a jingle of ankle bells, the masqueraders were gone, shuffling down the road and followed by a mob of laughing children. "Merry Christmas!" we called out. Our 1974 Christmas in Nsukka, Nigeria, had begun.

Maybe it wouldn't be so bad after all, I thought. Homesickness had clouded my holiday spirit for days. My multitude of fears in bringing our family to this far-off land, ten thousand miles away from our home, had gradually dissipated since our arrival that fall. The Igbo people had welcomed us with such hospitality! We were fortunate to live among the Igbos of southeastern Nigeria, as there are unusually large numbers of Christians in that area. Most people in the north are Muslims, and most from the west belong to tribal religions.

The culture shock of being whites in a country filled with one hundred thousand blacks also eased as we became more accustomed to curious onlookers wherever we went. Strangers would touch our daughter's long blond hair. Women in the marketplace would look at me, look at my children, and then say, "You did well." My husband, Lorry, enjoyed his teaching assignment at the University of Nigeria as a Fulbright lecturer, the purpose for our one-year visit to this unusual land.

But as Christmas approached, my homesickness increased. I missed the traditions of Christmastime in Utah—the fragrance of freshly cut Christmas trees; the tastes of mincemeat pie, roast turkey and dressing; the gathering of the extended family; the beauty of falling snow and brisk cold weather. I missed our two oldest sons, Todd serving as a missionary in New Zealand and Bryce continuing his studies in music at the University of Utah.

Oh, we did manage to assemble a small, tabletop tinsel Christmas tree decorated with tissue paper chains, and the children had put out a handsome nativity scene handcrafted by thorn carvers and had hung paper chains on the wall. We had seen the Nigerian equivalent of Santa Claus, a lean, white-bearded Nigerian wearing a red shirt, riding in a Land Rover and tossing hard candies to the children at Kent's primary school. Santa didn't seem to fit their culture. This Western myth, like soft drinks, yeast breads, candy, and Levis, had probably filtered into the African culture from ours, I speculated, although we had no radio, television, or telephone.

What I didn't miss were crowded malls and throngs of Christmas shoppers. The pressure of parties and programs was gone. The stress of baking and cooking holiday goodies and then overeating was gladly given up. The open market at Nsukka, where we did our shopping, was much the same as usual during the holiday season. The food on our table was about the same on Christmas Day as it was on any other day of the week—nourishing and healthful and consisting of fresh fruit, greens, fish or poultry, and pounded yams.

In addition to weekly worship services held in our home, we joined our Nigerian friends during the holidays, attending religious services in large attractive buildings on campus of both Catholic and Protestant faiths, where appropriate music and messages from the pulpit commemorated the birth of Jesus Christ. Attending these services were students, faculty members, and townspeople dressed both in Western clothes and colorful native costumes—

the women wearing elegant dresses, wrappers, and turbans, and men in embroidered shirts or nicely tailored suits. Their music was enthusiastic and rousing.

A Christmas pageant was presented by students at the campus theater building. The nativity scene included a white baby doll as Jesus, with the other actors native Nigerians. I wept as we sang with them the familiar carols and heard the choir present an excerpt from Handel's *Messiah*.

Another colorful church our family liked to attend, an apostolic church, was located in the bush area surrounding the college town. This congregation met in a simple one-room structure with thatched roof, plastered walls, and packed, red dirt floors. We appreciated the glassless windows that allowed air to move through the room as we sat on crude wooden benches with the others, usually women sitting on one side and men on the other. Clucking chickens punctuated the sermon, and barefoot children ran in and out of open doorways. The drone of flies and goats bleating blended with the soft movement of hand fans. We were moved by the lively sermons and drum-and-gong accompaniments to simple dancing and fervent singing. But no matter what denomination, these Nigerian Christians were deeply devoted and committed to unselfish service and family cohesiveness as they celebrated Christmas.

There would be no snow in this land of perpetual summer so near the equator. Christmas fell during the harmattan season, distinguished by hazy gray skies and dry windy weather. It did not rain a drop from early November until late April. The harmattan winds off the Sahara Desert dropped temperatures into the low seventies. We needed thin blankets at night, purchased from the local open market.

Our Christmas shopping took place on a road trip from Nsukka to Lagos. We chose gifts for each other, native art such as bronze figures cast by a man on the streets of Benin, wood-carvings from a peddler in Onitsha, and a talking drum my husband had bartered from a Hausa we met in the countryside.

More than their own gifts, the children were excited about the gifts they had purchased for our Nigerian steward, Cyprian Ugwu, and his wife Veronica, and their babies, Innocence and Celestine. We had grown fond of this little family who lived in quarters in the corner of our small compound, or yard. Every morning except Sunday, Cyprian would softly pad into our kitchen and begin his day's work by preparing breakfast for our family. He killed and plucked chickens, swept and scrubbed floors, boiled drinking water, washed vegetables in chlorine water, scrubbed clothes and hung them on bushes to dry, and interpreted the Igbo language and culture for us. At first we prepared lemon meringue pies, spaghetti, and other Western foods. We soon learned it was too difficult to purchase the provisions for these dishes and instead ate more healthy Nigerian food such as *egusi* soup and pounded yam.

Kent played with the Ugwu children in the compound when he wasn't attending school. Our four children were enrolled in Nigerian public schools, each of them the only American and *on-yocha* (white person) in their classes. The three older children wore white uniforms, and Kent wore a uniform of navy blue shorts and a checked shirt.

Our children noticed that Celestine and Innocence didn't have shoes to wear, even though Nigerian children often go barefoot. They wanted their little friends to have shoes, so they traveled to the marketplace and purchased small leather sandals, wrapped them in brown paper, and presented them to the Ugwu children on Christmas Eve. The gift was appreciated as Cyprian repeated, "Thank you! Thank you! God bless you! God bless you!" Celestine and Innocence loved the sandals and wore them continuously from that day on.

As Christmas Day drew to a close, I realized how happy I was. Our own family had never felt such a spirit of unity and joy. What a privilege it was for us to be in this land and learn of our black brothers and sisters! We came to appreciate the love and unity of their families, the sacrifice and importance they place on education, and the desire they have for peace and understanding in the world.

It was in this country, so different from my own, that I began to realize how the Savior must love and accept all people throughout the world, no matter what color their skin, what clothes they wear, what kind of house they live in, or what language they speak. His message of love and peace was equally important to my Nigerian friends as to my friends back home. My all-white mentality had changed to a kaleidoscope of different colors and an appreciation of the beauty of the Nigerian people. This was the message I received that Christmas—the Christmas I remember best.

CHRISTMAS FROM THE PAST

Betty Jo Jepsen

Christmas in a small rural community in Idaho is not just a memory, it really reflects a way of life. As I reminisce, the season is all wrapped up in lots of snow, the school Christmas play, family get-togethers, special goodies, the music, tree-cutting, and the annual dance at the church on the evening of December 25.

I do not remember material gifts given or received, but I do remember how I felt. The feelings unique to Christmas began slowly with a tingle of excitement when we were able to use stacks of red and green construction paper to make chains for decorating every nook and cranny of our wonderful old school building in Mink Creek.

About that same time our classes began practicing the music of the season. Our school had four rooms, each with two grades and a teacher. Each grade had ten to twelve students, bringing the total studentbody to about eighty. The school Christmas production presented on the stage of the church building next door was a major event in the community. The speaking parts were divided among the oldest students in

the school, but each student had an important part and costume, even if their role was as a member of the chorus.

For several weeks before the program, we were motivated to work very hard on our academic subjects in order to spend the afternoon practicing our parts. The windup dancing doll, the soldiers, the angels, and the lighted tree seem to have been standard features in my memory, all lovingly presented in the final performance for our parents on the evening of the last day of school before Christmas vacation.

My memories of Christmas include a feeling of anticipation and excitement as Christmas Eve approached. I remember watching for the lights in the barn to go out. I knew then that the cows had been milked and the other animals put to bed for the night. Soon our celebration could begin. The tree had to be in the same location every year. There was only one electrical outlet in the living room of our big farmhouse. The great thing about that was that when the tree was plugged in, everything else in the room had to be off, making the tree the absolute center of our attention.

Our washroom was an unheated addition to our house with a concrete floor and a drain. This room served to keep cold a case of bottled sodas and a case of oranges for our enjoyment during the holiday season.

On the evening of December 25, Mink Creek Ward always hosted a dance with a band. The band played from the stage. The hall was decorated with trees and lights. People came from all around the area to enjoy this dance. Our house was across the street from the chapel. As a child too young to participate, I watched from the front window as cars arrived, often in a downfall of snow, and tried to identify those I knew as they rushed into the ward dance hall.

When I began to attend MIA, I was able to go to the dance. Fathers twirled their daughters dressed in new Christmas frocks around the floor. Couples celebrated the season by exchanging partners and wishing each new partner a fine holiday season. The music was loud, the hall really overcrowded, the spirit wonderful, and the memories glorious. I am not sure what the janitor sprinkled on the floor, but it allowed my feet to barely touch it as I was gently guided around the hall. Young and old bumped and greeted each other as they danced. My memories of Christmas are all tied up in the school, home, and church activities of the season. It was a warm, comfortable way to celebrate.

I relish a special Christmas story that my Grandmother Orial Brown told me.

If she had lived, she would have been one hundred years old in 1990. She was the third born of twelve children and the oldest girl. Grandmother Brown was a small person. She often told of having to stand on a chair to wash the dishes and mix the bread. She reminded those of us who complained about housework that she had done the washing for a family of twelve brothers and sisters in a big tub and heated the water on the stove.

Orial's mother, my great-grandmother, was often not in good health (having carried twelve children in twenty-two years), and it was necessary for Grandmother to help out a great deal with the work of the house. Great-grandmother Taylor also left my grandmother with responsibility for the family while she ministered to neighbors during sickness.

My great-grandfather, Joseph Lake Taylor, was a farmer in Grant, Jefferson County, Idaho. When Orial was about twelve years old, her father made a special trip into town to purchase gifts for the family Christmas. As her father returned home late on the eve of Christmas and made plans to wrap and place the gifts for his children on the tree, he realized that he had forgotten to purchase a gift for Orial. He was devastated, but with the lateness of the hour, and considering the long journey by horse and buggy into town where most of the businesses were now closed, he had no choice except to try to explain his mistake to his daughter.

Orial's father knew his daughter

well. Of all his children, she would be the most understanding. She was pure in heart and always gave willingly for brothers and sisters in the family. As my grandmother recalled the events of that Christmas for us, she often admited that she had felt bad about being left out because Christmas was such a special event for her. In fact, she said she found a quiet place and cried a little, but she didn't want anyone to see her. She knew her father had not overlooked her deliberately.

Grandmother said, "I could understand how it could happen—there were so many of us." By then there was Lorin, Ira, Orial, Grace, Del, Darwin, Lawrence, Dorthulia, and Vaughan. She rejoiced in the gifts of the other family members. My great-grandfather went into town the day after Christmas, a full day's trip, to purchase a gift for his oldest daughter. Grandmother treasured the little autograph book she received belatedly. She kept if for many years, but could vividly describe it as she related the story to her children and grandchildren.

I have always felt proud to be a descendant of a woman whose inner goodness would be so evident that her father had total faith that she would be understanding and forgiving of his oversight, even at such a special time as Christmas.

THE CHRISTMAS MOON

Don Lind

Some aspects of Christmas are always the same. And some parts change from year to year. For example, every Christmas we have snow. Frequently the snow has to be imaginary because most of our married life we have lived in too warm a climate for real snow. But in my mind, it wouldn't be Christmas unless I at least felt there was going to be snow.

One thing that actually is the same from year to year is gathering the family around the Christmas tree on Christmas Eve to read the story of that first Christmas from the book of Luke. For our family it would not be Christmas without that. And every year when we finish reading from the Bible, we also read the story "Why the Chimes Rang." This tradition started in my parents' home when I was a boy. We had heard it so many times that when my parents were on a mission in Australia, and they needed a story for a branch Christmas party, my father could recite it verbatim from memory.

Every year we put our presents around the tree with the same time-honored procedure. Each family member in turn, from the youngest to the oldest, gathers their gifts from their hiding places and, as they approach the room where the family waits around the tree, rings a set of old sleigh bells. That is the signal that everyone must close their eyes while the presents are artistically arranged under the tree. When the bells are rung the second time, everyone is allowed to open their eyes and look at the grand display. Although it is an open secret that there is a lot of peeking, the surprised oohs and aahs sound just as genuine year after year.

Some things in our family tradition change slowly. I don't think we do nearly as much caroling as we did when more of the children were at home. And some things are also added from time to time. As my father's birthday falls in the holiday season, we decided to do something uniquely Swedish one year. We made decorations for the tree out of long, carefully cut wood shavings. There were scrolls and stars and little trees and dolls, all made out of strips of wood planed from the edge of a board.

And for Dad's seventy-fifth birthday we started our version of the "Santa Lucia" tradition. Early that Christmas morning our daughters awakened the other family members with the old traditional Swedish song and served them sweet buns and hot wassail. One daughter even wore the historic crown of flaming candles in her hair. Over the years we have kept the singing and the food but have eliminated the candles. We worry too much about setting someone's hair on fire.

While there are many similarities among most Christmases of the past, some holiday seasons have been noticeably different from the others. This may have been because a family member was on a mission and would not be with us that year. Once it was because all of the family was ill and we had to adjust the schedule until we felt better.

One Christmas that will always remain vivid in my memory is the Christmas of 1968. Along with the family portion of that holiday, there was some special history that I will always remember. At that Christmastime I had been an astronaut for over two years. All that time we had been working feverishly to get Americans to the moon before the Russians got there.

It was almost Christmas when the Apollo spacecraft was ready to fly. As our family paused amid our holiday preparations and breathlessly watched on television as the giant Saturn 5 rocket roared into action on December 21, we knew it was a historic day. Frank Borman, Jim Lovell, and Bill An-

ders, who were onboard Apollo 8, were finally on their way toward lunar orbit. The United States was going to be the first nation to orbit the moon after all!

There were many firsts on that magnificent 590,000-mile trip to the moon and back. Never before had man ventured so far away, or left his home planet for another. Never had we tried to operate a spacecraft so far from ground support. Never had we operated out of telemetry contact with the earth while we were behind another planetary body. We felt well prepared as this mission began, but we also knew there was something very special about this flight.

I pictured my friends Frank, Jim, and Bill looking back in awe at our beautiful blue world growing smaller and smaller as they sped deeper into space. I could recall clearly how I had felt as a naval aviator as our aircraft carrier sailed under the Golden Gate Bridge heading into the Pacific near the end of the Korean War. As my homeland gradually disappeared from view over the horizon, a feeling of deep love and longing filled the empty place in my stomach. I knew the Apollo crew was having the same feelings of loneliness and nostalgia, but in an even more dramatic way.

From their spacecraft window, however, the earth was still visible, and the view back toward the home planet was spectacular. They commented on it frequently. As they got closer to the moon, Frank informed mission control in Houston that it appeared that they were headed directly toward the center of the moon. With a chuckle, CapCom said they would recheck the trajectory calculation.

However at the proper moment, the Apollo capsule correctly skimmed past the edge of the moon and, pulled by the strength of lunar gravity, whipped around to the unseen back side. Out of sight of the earth, the crew fired the spacecraft engine to slow down so that their momentum would not fling them back into the darkness of space. As they settled their spacecraft safely into an orbit around the moon, it was well into the holiday season celebrating the anniversary of our Savior's birth. I imagine much of the world paused in their holiday rush to marvel at what wonderful things the Lord was permitting man to accomplish. And the crew members felt that, because their great journey had happened to occur during the Christmas season, it was appropriate to acknowledge the Lord's hand in this event. So on Christmas Eve of 1968, as they orbited the moon, the Apollo 8 astronauts read outloud on their worldwide telecast the account of the Creation from the Bible.

"In the beginning God created the heavens and the earth.

"And the earth was without form, and void; and darkness was upon the face of the deep. . . .

"And God said, Let there be light. . . .

"And God said, Let the waters under the heaven be gathered together unto one place, and let the dry land appear. . . .

"And God made two great lights; the greater light to rule the day, and the lesser light to rule the night. . . .

"And God saw that it was good." (Genesis 1:1–3, 9, 16, 18.)

That year, in addition to reading the account of the Savior's birth on Christmas Eve, our family also read again the story of the Creation. Then my wife and children and I went out in our backyard and looked up at the moon and marveled that we actually knew the three brave men who were at that moment orbiting that bright lunar sphere. As we shivered in wonder, we read by the light of the full moon David's prayer in the eighth Psalm: "When I consider thy heavens, the work of thy fingers, the moon and the stars, which thou hast ordained; What is man, that thou are mindful of him? and the son of man, that thou visitest him? For thou hast . . . crowned him with glory and honour." (Psalm 8:3–5.)

After we had read these words, we had a family circle hug and sang together one of our favorite Christmas hymns: "Oh holy night, the stars are brightly shining. It is the night of our dear Savior's birth."

For our family, Christmas 1968 will always be remembered with grateful and wondering awe.

GIVING AND RECEIVING

Kathleen H. Barnes

It was December 23—just two days before Christmas. In our family it was a tradition on this day to organize a Christmas activity that included others. We'd had some wonderful experiences in years past, including distributing clothing among the local Asian population, visiting widows, or providing Christmas for a needy family.

This year we had decided to visit Wanet. Wanet was a young man who lived in Berkeley, California, and had been attending the university there. We didn't know him personally, only of him. We knew that he was a quadriplegic confined to his bed, alone and without family.

I called him a few days prior to our visit to ask if we could stop by and wish him a Merry Christmas. He was gracious, though he may have felt a little uncomfortable welcoming strangers into his home.

As the hour of our visit approached, we began to feel apprehensive. Our children were particularly concerned, wondering if it would be uncomfortable or if it might even be rude to present ourselves to a perfect stranger. And so it was with some anxiety that we climbed the stairs that evening and approached his apartment door.

Wanet's loud "come in" welcomed us, and we opened the door on a room that resembled a refined hospital. The hospital bed, the medicines, and the machines all signaled that this indeed was a very sick young man.

After brief introductions, we began to talk. He wanted to know all about us, our family, our Christmas traditions, our experiences, our background; and in turn, we asked about his story.

It was 1968 in Tempe, Arizona. Wanet had just graduated from high school. He had joined the Church a couple of years prior to that time and was enrolled at Arizona State University. It was a time of unrest in the country. Robert Kennedy and Martin Luther King had been assassinated. Spacecraft were orbiting the moon, and the United States was heavily involved in Vietnam. There was a lot of pressure on male students during those years, because if they didn't maintain their grade averages, they would become eligible for the draft. Campus demonstrations and riots in opposition to the war were continually erupting.

Wanet did not want to go to war. He had his sights on medical school and as a result threw himself into his studies at the exclusion of almost everything else in his life. He withdrew from friends, from social gatherings, and even from the Church.

And then in 1974 he was involved in a terrible automobile accident that left him paralyzed from the neck down. In a matter of minutes his world turned upside down. His future seemed to vanish, and he found himself in an empty chasm with no way out. Even those close to him seemed to disappear, including his wife. He had nothing to hold on to, nothing to count on. He was lost and alone. His life became a maze of hospitals, infection, respiratory ailments, pneumonia, and skin deterioration. For a year he survived an endless loneliness filled with illness. Perhaps the only thing that kept him going was his natural curiosity regarding world conditions and what would happen next.

In 1975 he moved to Berkeley and was able to enroll with the hope of eventually getting into a Ph.D program in neurophysiology. Somewhere in the back of his mind was the hope that maybe he could find a cure for his debilitating condition, but declining health prevented him from staying in school very long. He didn't know from one week to the next if he would be in or out of the hospital. It was so difficult. It seemed to be impossible to do anything but just exist.

It was at this low point in his life that he became acquainted with Brad Robison. Brad called one evening and introduced himself as a home teacher. He wondered why Wanet hadn't been out to church. Wanet responded with a quick, "Well, my legs just don't seem to want to go there on Sunday."

"Yeah," Brad responded, "a lot of people feel that way." Brad went on to ask if he could come over and visit, so arrangements were made. When Brad arrived, he was more than surprised to find that Wanet's legs really didn't want to cooperate.

This was the beginning of a meaningful friendship. Brad continued to visit, but for two years their visits centered on Brad's pre-med studies, Wanet's needs, and just things in general. There were times when Wanet rejected the friendship and would refuse to talk, but eventually the trust grew and Brad began to once again introduce Wanet to the gospel.

Old feelings stirred in Wanet—feelings that were related to that happy period in his life when as a new convert he had embraced the gospel. He started to think of the bishop who fellowshipped him into the church, of the bishop's family who had loved him so much. He remembered working side by side with the bishop on his farm, and those feelings of love and warmth began to grow.

One night, as he struggled to sort out his thoughts, he decided to call that bishop. As a result of that conversation, the family sent him a Book of Mormon and Wanet began once again to become converted to the gospel. His heart began to turn to the Lord, and a peace entered his soul.

Brad's visits continued, and together they explored the gospel. Brad would record sacrament meetings and bring them to Wanet. Those tiny seeds, planted many years before, were once again being nourished and were beginning to sprout and grow.

For the first time since the accident, Wanet began to focus on the goodness of life and the blessings that were his.

But then another disaster struck. Wanet was hospitalized for surgery. While he was recovering, his van and many of his possessions, including all of his money, were stolen. He was left with nothing except debt. In deep despair he lay in his bed wondering what to do. It was at that point that Brad walked through the door. "I knew in a moment what I needed to do," he said, and asked Brad to call for the bishop. Through the bishop he was able to take care of his immediate needs and to begin the slow process of financial recovery.

From that time on, Wanet grew in the gospel. He began to find the strength to carry on, and he even started to work toward going to the temple.

That humbling pre-Christmas night,

as we sat in that small room, we too sensed a feeling of peace and resolve. We were strengthened by the story we had heard. We closed the evening by watching videos of Wanet playing football in days now gone. We marveled at his ability to talk about the past and, now, about the future. He had learned so much and now was teaching us. He reminded us that there are costly mistakes that one can make. He had made one when he had gone on a ride one night with a friend. He didn't like the way the friend was driving and had wanted to offer to drive. But he hadn't, and now he lay paralyzed. "Learn from me," he said. "Listen to the still small voice. Avoid circumstances that can lead to sin or disaster. Stay close to your Heavenly Father so that the winds of the world will not buffet you about."

As we left his apartment that night, we were filled with gratitude for legs that would take us down stairs, for arms that could swing in the breeze, for the sensation of cold air blowing on our faces. We were grateful for this young man's courage and strength. We were buoyed by his testimony and his resilient spirit. The fear we'd felt as we approached his apartment had been replaced with friendship, for in that quiet room we had found a new friend. "Merry Christmas, Wanet," we whispered, "and thank you for awakening in us the real spirit of this season—gratitude for the gift of life."

THE GLORIOUS GIFT

Jaroldeen Edwards

When you have twelve children, your store of treasured Christmas memories is like Santa Claus's sack—full to the brim. As I open my sackful of remembrances, they all come tumbling out, one after the other, bright, complex, funny, sad—like a jumble of Christmas toys—everything from clowns to angels. I see the years of Christmases past like a kaleidoscope of memories with the glass spinning too quickly.

I remember the Christmas in Holden Green, in Cambridge, Massachusetts, when my husband, Weston, was completing his last year as a graduate student at Harvard. We had four children, and our total Christmas budget (in those years we actually lived within our budget) was fifty dollars. Our "Christmas" arrived in one single large box of things ordered from the *Sears Roebuck* catalog. Weston spent the entire night of Christmas Eve, from bedtime until the dawn of Christmas morning, putting together the heavy cardboard sink, stove, and refrigerator that were the gifts for our three little girls. The assembly instructions had been written in English by the Japanese company that made the product. They would probably have been more useful if they had been written in Japanese!

I remember the year we finally caved in to the importuning of our four-year-old daughter, Christine. All she wanted was a "pet" for Christmas. We got her a lovely little ginger-colored kitten. She named the animal "Queenie."

It quickly became apparent that Queenie was a neurotic animal. The cat could not be tamed! Christine would carry the kitten gently in her arms, crooning loving words, while the cat would be raking her tender arms and hands with its claws. The poor child looked like she had been thrown into a raspberry patch and told to find her way out. We took the kitten to the veterinarian, and the cat bit the vet. He told us that occasionally an aberrant animal is born, and there was nothing we could do about it.

Nevertheless, the memory of the unwavering love Christine gave that very unloveable cat is one of my treasured Christmas memories. To be so constant! What an example! However, several years later, when we were living in

81

Connecticut, I overheard one of my older children say to one of the younger ones, "Don't ever ask for a pet for Christmas. Mother will just buy you a bird feeder!" I laughed, because it dawned on me that for three years running I had bought bird feeders for the children to hang in the woods behind our house. "Enjoy the animals in their *natural* setting," had become my motherly encouragement.

Each year we put on a homegrown Christmas pageant, and the memories of these are legion. My best Christmas pageant memory occurred when we had moved into our first real home. We had invited some families for Christmas Eve dinner, and to share in our pageant.

I was just putting the finishing touches on the buffet, and the guests were due to arrive, when powerful fumes wafted through the kitchen. I quickly ran down the basement stairs to the family room. The smell was almost overwhelming. Turpentine! In the workroom under the stairs I found the source. Our eight-year-old son, Charles, had made a manger to surprise us.

It was a wonderful manger. He had designed it, hammered it together, and gathered hay to fill it; but the wood had come from some old orange crates, and there was advertising on the side. At the last minute Charles had decided to make the manger "perfect" by painting it. The paint had spilled on the floor, and he had poured turpentine on the paint to clean it up. The odor made your eyes water!

Even after we mopped up the turpentine, the overpowering fumes continued to seep through the house as the guests arrived. No one could eat much, and we all watched the pageant while sort of gasping for breath. My twelve-year-old daughter, the "producer" of the pageant, kept reminding Mary, Joseph and the angels, in a loud stage whisper, "Don't touch the manger. It's wet paint!"

The guests left early. Many of them had tears in their eyes—I'm not sure whether they were tears of laughter, allergy, or emotion. But when I think of that Christmas, I remember a little eight-year-old boy who loved the story of the Christ Child's birth so much that he tried to create the perfect gift.

Of all my myriad memories, my most treasured one is the memory of the Christmas when we *did* receive the perfect gift, and with it came an eternal understanding and an unfaltering commitment.

We were living in a wonderful suburb of New York City, Short Hills, New Jersey. It was a small town with lovely tree-lined, winding streets, great schools, and good neighbors. We were one of only a handful of Mormon families in that town.

Our pediatrician was a man named Dr. Kearney. He was Catholic and had nine children of his own, and so he was very supportive of our family of seven children, with an eighth on the way. He was a man who respected children. He was quick, decisive, and insightful. If he didn't think mothers

82

were taking their responsibilities seriously enough, he could be impatient with them; but he was *never* impatient with a child. It was as though he saw himself as the champion of children, and he was always on their side. Not that he pampered children. He was definitely not a "kootchy-koo" kind of doctor with babies. Older children were expected to behave well and bravely when they were in his office, but Dr. Kearney earned their good behavior through mutual respect, not through anger or disapproval.

Among other things I liked about him was the fact that he was one of those rare doctors who will listen to mothers and take what they say seriously. He would often say to a young mother, "You are the best observer of your child. If you sense there is something wrong, there probably is, and we will find out what it is, or lay your concerns to rest." He gave me confidence in myself and in him.

It was the middle of December, and Short Hills looked like an engraving from Currier and Ives. The snow-covered trees, the tall, gabled homes, the brightly-scarfed children sleigh-riding in the park, and the Christmas tree lights sparkling in windows in the early dark gave everything a festive glow.

I was expecting my eighth baby in six weeks. Carolyn, our youngest child, was eighteen months old. She was a sweet, dainty little girl, with feet that seemed to dance instead of walk and a smile of such open brightness that she seemed to carry sunlight within her.

(Oh, how can you describe the face of any loved child? It is so rare and precious that words simply fail. I used to look at my children clustered around me with their eyes on mine and their hearts as open as their glorious, innocent faces, and I felt I had stepped into some celestial garden.)

Two weeks before Christmas, with no symptoms at all, Carolyn began to run a fever. When I woke up at two o'clock in the morning to check on her, she was burning up. I called Dr. Kearney in alarm, and he, hearing the fear in my voice, came to our home within fifteen minutes. He was still wearing his pajamas under his suit pants. I could see the flannel fabric sticking out from under his cuffs.

The night was bitterly cold and snowing. He wrapped Carolyn in a heavy quilt, my husband carried her to the car, and we drove through the dark, empty streets to the hospital.

Then followed the long days and nights that so many parents have endured. The tests, the medications, the nurses and doctors, the tubes and needles, and the weak, silent, golden child. It is a litany familiar to any family who has had a hospitalized child.

My husband took his vacation. Day after day we took turns sitting by her in the little bed, trying somehow to keep the family going, making endless trips to and from the hospital, and continuing with half-hearted preparations for Christmas.

Finally the problem was diagnosed

and a sophisticated and somewhat experimental course of medication was begun. "The bacteria have not reacted to the other antibiotics," Dr. Kearney explained to us. "This new stuff we're trying should do the trick, but she won't be out of the woods until she has been free from fever for forty-eight hours. We just can't seem to get that fever down."

Through the two weeks since Carolyn had been put in the hospital, Dr. Kearney had watched over her like a bulldog. When he was in his office he would remain in touch with the hospital by phone. He did not express his concern to us in words, but the intense seriousness of his tired face told us volumes.

In those days parents were not allowed to remain overnight with their children. We were expected to leave the hospital at 11:00 P.M., and we were permitted to return for the day at 9:00 A.M. On the night before Christmas Eve, as we prepared to leave the hospital, Dr. Kearney came in to check Carolyn one last time before going home. He looked as weary as it is possible for a human being to look. Gently he examined her and her chart, then he turned to us with a sigh.

"She is still running a low-grade fever," he said. "I feel there is improvement, but until we break this fever I can't be sure." His voice was discouraged. We knew this medication was our last chance.

Tears came to my eyes. "She won't be home for Christmas." It was a state-ment, not a question. Doctor Kearney just shook his head.

Christmas Eve day Weston stayed at the hospital while I finished buying a few last gifts for the children. We tried to keep things as normal as possible, and so we held our family pageant late that night when Weston came home. Then we tucked our six precious children into bed. They were worried for Carolyn, and missed her very much, but they were young, and the excitement of Christmas still bubbled within them.

After the children were asleep, Weston and I went down to the living room. We carried the sacks of presents from all the closets, nooks, and crannies where they were hidden and began to place gifts and toys at each child's place. I took the six stockings and started filling them with candies, tiny toys, and little individual treats. Almost as though it had been another person, another time, and another place, I remembered the joy I had felt just a few weeks earlier as I had purchased or made each gift. Now I could feel nothing at all, and Christmas just seemed like a dreadful ordeal which must be faced for the sake of the children.

My heart felt like lead. It was all I could do to continue my task. As I opened one of the bags, I lifted out a delicate blue dress with lace trim and ruffled petticoats, so small it almost looked like a doll's dress. I had bought the dress with delight early in December for Carolyn's Christmas. I held the beautiful dress in my hands and, in despair, wondered if she would ever wear it. Without control, I put the soft fabric to my face and wept.

The next morning the children were up before dawn, and we watched as they opened their gifts and emptied their stockings. They tried valiantly to be exuberant and natural. The younger ones succeeded, and the rest of us tried to join in their delight. Even though the room was full of beloved family, and even though arms were full of the finest toys which money could buy, and even though we sat in a beautiful room full of comfortable furniture, safe from cold and storm, and even though our lives were surrounded by loving friends and relatives, as Weston and I sat side by side in the midst of all that joy and plenty, our hearts yearned after one bright, tiny spirit who was missing. Without that last sweet child the circle was incomplete and our happiness was hollow. The older children felt it too. Only "one" missing—but the room felt empty.

It was almost time for Weston to leave for the hospital. It was eight o'clock in the morning, and the winter sun was dawning weakly. The phone rang, and I went to answer it.

It was Dr. Kearney. "Don't leave for the hospital," he said. "I'll be at your door in a few minutes. I have something for you." He hung up before I could say a word.

"Was he leaving his own dear family on Christmas morning to bring us a present?" I wondered outloud. "He

didn't even give me a chance to ask about Carolyn. He probably hasn't had a chance to call the hospital yet this morning."

I went into the living room and told Weston about the call. We didn't have more than a minute or two to speculate. The doorbell rang, and we hurried to answer it. There on our doorstep stood Dr. Kearney. His hat was jammed over his ears and he was muffled in a thick scarf. In his arms was the quilt in which we had carried Carolyn to the hospital those many long days ago.

He stepped into the hallway and unwrapped the quilt, and a darling, bright-eyed little girl held out her arms and said, "Mommy!"

"Merry Christmas!" said Dr. Kearney, with a great smile in his solemn eyes. "I went over to the hospital early this morning, and it was incredible! Her fever broke sometime during the night. She may need to go back, but I figure you're the best nurse she could have. So here she is. I thought you probably needed each other for Christmas."

I couldn't speak. The feelings in my heart were too poignant, too profound, too enormous. "Glory" is the only word that begins to describe them.

Dr. Kearney, that splendid, caring, righteous man, hurried home to take his own waiting family to Catholic Mass where they could pray together. We took our precious baby daughter into the heart of our home. United, all together again, we knelt in the completed circle of our family and prayed together.

How do you begin to thank the Lord for such gifts? For men like Dr. Kearney who really care? For each dear child? For a strong, valiant husband who magnifies his priesthood? For the gospel? For understanding? The list is as endless as the circle of a family.

As we carried Carolyn into the room and the family clustered around her, their eyes shining with love, I understood as never before the parable of the shepherd and the sheep. I knew that as many children as we would be privileged to have, *that* would be how many we must strive to bring back to our heavenly home. If even one is missing, the loss is beyond measure. What a glorious gift! Not just the return of our blessed baby daughter, but eternal conviction and a lifetime commitment to do all in our power to keep the circle forever complete.

MY MOST MEMORABLE CHRISTMAS

Barbara W. Winder

It was twelve. Our family had felt the strain of the great Depression, and now we were helping with the war effort as our country was plunged deep into World War II. A newly developed park adjacent to the creek was the delight of our community. During the cold winter of 1943, local residents decided to flood a portion of the park, creating an ice pond where the young people could skate.

More than anything else, I wanted shoe ice skates for Christmas. It seemed to me at that point that nothing would be more perfect than being able to go skating with all the other children and youth in our neighborhood. But I was old enough to realize that the financial circumstances in our family made this dream impossible.

Somehow, and I don't know to this day quite how, my parents managed to get me that wonderful pair of skates! I wanted them to know of my appreciation, and I wanted their sacrifice to be worthwhile.

There were no formal instructors to teach us. We had to help each other. We learned much more than just skat-

ing. There were the usual races and competitions, but the camaraderie of sharing and teaching others our new-found skills made us more like team-mates than competitors. As we assisted one another we learned to love each other, and lasting bonds of friendship were formed.

During those experiences I also developed a love for nature as I enjoyed the wintery beauty of those clear, cold January nights, with nothing but the moon as our light.

I wonder if my father and mother knew their sacrifice would not only help me learn a skill, but also learn valuable lessons in relationships, lessons of sharing, of serving, and of feeling the joy that comes from cooperation and accomplishment. With hindsight, I now see that the skates were a blessing in many more ways than I then realized, and in more ways than my parents had maybe even hoped for.

When a gift is given, whether it be a longed-for pair of skates, a treasured book, or the hand of friendship, sacrifice is often a part of that gift. It is important that we not treat our gifts lightly. There are also heavenly gifts and talents bestowed upon each of us by a loving Father, given that we might bless and edify one another.

Ultimate sacrifice was certainly pres-ent in the greatest of all gifts. As we reflect on what that means, Christmas is made more meaningful and more memorable as we serve Him who so generously gave.

CHRISTMAS MEMORIES

Joseph Fielding McConkie

Ah, that memories and feelings could be hung on a Christmas tree like ornaments and tinsel! How marvelous it would be if instead of lacing the branches of our Christmas trees with colored lights we could make them sparkle with the glow of the special lessons that the Christmas season teaches so well. Three of our nine children have been born during Christmas week. Near countless times we have heard well-meaning people say, "Oh, what an awful time to have a baby!"

How strange—too busy commemorating the birth of Christ to have a child of our own? Yet, no one has ever said to us, "Oh, what a wonderful time to have a child!" My mind returns to bitter winter days in England. As missionaries we called on hundreds of homes in December, asking if we could share a brief message about the Savior with them. Again and again we heard the words, "I'm sorry, we're getting ready for Christmas."

Perhaps the birth of our children during the holiday season has kept us from getting too busy, and it has certainly enriched the Christmas tradition in our family. The cast of characters in our traditional portrayal of the nativity story has often included a real mother-to-be, one "heavy with child," and in other years a precious newborn to lay in our own makeshift manger.

In large measure our family traditions are a reenactment of boyhood memories—getting up Christmas morning, dressing, making our beds, having something to eat (in the vain hope that we wouldn't stuff ourselves with Christmas candy), lining up according to age (there were eight of us), waiting for Dad to go into the living room to turn on the Christmas lights and see if Santa had really come, and then hearing his manifestation of surprise that Santa had indeed been there.

About mid-morning, Granddaddy Smith and Aunt Jessy would arrive. Everyone was to be hugged and kissed—by the man others thought to be the stern apostle—and then he would give each of us a new silver dollar.

After their visit, we were all loaded in the car so we could visit our Mc-Conkie grandparents. The last of those visits was particularly memorable. Granddaddy McConkie had been ill for some time. At the conclusion of our visit, Granddaddy said he had something very important to tell us. We all gathered around, and even the young ones were quiet.

I don't remember all he said that day, but some of his words I will never forget. "I am about to die," he began. "I don't know yet what my assignment will be in the spirit world, but this much I do know: when I die I will not cease to love you; I will not cease to be concerned about you; I will not cease to pray for you; and I will not cease to labor in your behalf." A few weeks later Oscar W. McConkie died. Things have happened in the family since that day that have evidenced Granddaddy has not forgotten his Christmas promise.

It was not many years ago that we shared our last Christmas with my own father, Elder Bruce R. McConkie. Since Dad was coming down to Provo on Christmas Day to speak to the missionaries at the Missionary Training Center, we were able to get him and Mother to join our family for Christmas dinner.

There was nothing that Dad loved to do more than take the scriptures and tell the story of the birth of Christ. He wanted to speak to the missionaries for a couple of hours but knew that his strength was very limited.

That was the last meeting I ever went to with him. None of us realized the seriousness of his situation. He spoke for an hour and then sat down. The missionaries sang, and special musical numbers were rendered while he rested. He then stood and spoke a second hour. We left immediately after the closing prayer. Dad wanted to shake hands with each of the missionaries, but he just didn't have the energy.

We returned to our home. Dad immediately lay down on the floor to rest. Cold, he asked if I had a sweater he could borrow. I went to my closet where I found a sweater he had given me for Christmas more than twenty years before. I had never worn it. The sleeves were too long. Why I had kept it all those years I don't know. I suppose I hoped that my arms would grow. I took the sweater to Dad and said, "Merry Christmas." The fit was perfect. He laid back down and fell comfortably asleep while my wife and the girls completed the preparations for dinner.

Christmas dinners are always good in our home, but this was one especially so. As we ate, we took turns unwrapping treasured memories, laughing, and crying together. That evening when Dad left he kept that sweater. It was wrapped tightly around him. Dad never cared about gifts. No one could ever figure out what to give him. In recent years I had made it a practice at Christmas to present him with a manuscript I had written and ask him to review it for me. That seemed to please him more than a gift.

Still, there was something special in my being able to return that sweater to him. In some unspoken way it seemed to represent my desire to return to him all that was warm and good that I had received from him. Maybe returning things is what Christmas is all about.

For us, Christmas has represented life's cycles—we have witnessed birth, enjoyed family kinships, and had our final partings with loved ones. In it all we are learning that the best of Christmas is not just in giving, but in the giving back the best of what has been given to us.

A KALEIDOSCOPE OF CHRISTMAS

Norma B. Ashton

"Write about your most memorable Christmas" was the assignment. Somehow I couldn't single out a specific year. A kaleidoscope of small segments of many Christmases flashed before my eyes.

I love Christmas—the hustle and bustle, the cooking and candy-making and decorating the house from top to bottom, the laughter, the Christmas music, the lights and candles and gifts hidden under the beds or in closets.

One of our family traditions begins early on Christmas morning when my husband turns on the Christmas music. We all dress, make our beds, eat a good breakfast, and then line up according to height to march into the room where the tree lights twinkle, a fire burns in the fireplace, and gifts are in place under the tree. In the first years Mom and Dad brought up the rear. As time passed, to the delight of the children, each one finally got to stand behind Mother until she had to lead the procession.

The children sometimes moaned about beds, breakfast, and dishes, but after the simple chores were done and they had a substantial breakfast, they were free to eat anything they wanted and to do what they chose to do the rest of the day.

With a turn of the kaleidoscope I again see two little granddaughters dressed in Christmas red standing by the wheelchair of their ninety-year-old great-grandfather as we all gathered for Christmas Eve dinner. Hardly aware of the festivities going on around him, great-grandfather's head would nod as he dozed. Stephanie and Kellie each took one of his hands. As they tenderly patted them, Kellie said, "That's all right, Grandpa John. You sleep if you want to. We will take care of you." They stood guard with loving care. Instinctively they understood Ralph Waldo Emerson's statement, "The only gift is a portion of thyself."

Another picture is printed on the collage of Christmases past. Santa Claus usually found his way to our home after Christmas Eve dinner to remind us to be good and to leave a small gift for each. To the surprise of all, he twice asked Grandpa Marv to come and sit on his knee. As the wide-eyed children watched, he put a hundred dollar bill into Grandpa's hand and said, "As you travel throughout the world, look for some person who really needs help and give him this gift from Santa."

Those watching were reminded again of our Savior's words, "Inasmuch as ye have done it unto one of the least of these my brethren, ye have done it unto me (Matthew 25:40)."

And still another glimpse. In one of the early years of our marriage, I remember sitting on the floor amid open boxes and stacks of gift-wrapping, knowing all the gifts had been claimed by their owners. My husband walked over to me and held out an unwrapped shoebox, saying, "You haven't been very good this year, so Santa left you a "box of coal." Laughing, I reached for the box that was, indeed, so heavy I almost dropped it. I shall never forget my excitement and surprise when I found a complete set of sterling silver in my favorite pattern. My expectation of ever owning such a gift had been to acquire it piece by piece as we could afford it.

One of our favorite decorations is a beautiful hand-carved creche made by the monks of St. Joseph's carpenter shop high in the mountains of Taiwan. As the grandchildren see the creche in its usual place, they go to the stable and gently lift baby Jesus from the manger to see if he is still the same as last year and often say, "Happy Birthday, Baby Jesus."

As the kaleidoscope turns slowly from one year to the next, I again feel the warm feeling that comes as I am surrounded with family and loved ones both from within the family circle and from an extended circle of friends and neighbors. I feel the peace that comes from loving and being loved. There is a prayer of gratitude for a good family, great friends, for health and happiness, and for the privilege of being born in this wonderful land of America. I realize, however, that the sights, sounds, and feelings of Christmas are only as good as we make them. It is up to us. Each Christmas brings to me a renewed hope for peace on earth and goodwill toward men.

ROOTS OF CHRISTMAS JOY

Elaine Cannon

Each season, we children tirelessly moved the pieces of the nativity set back and forth like checkers across the creche, arranging and rearranging our manger scene with tenderness. I don't remember if the set was fine porcelain or simple celluloid, but to my brothers, sisters and me it was wonderful. It was our "Silent Night, Holy Night" scene that inevitably conjured up the spirit of that first Christmas.

First Christmas—a magic, telling phrase.

How well I remember the first Christmas in love when I received my diamond ring. Our first Christmas as newlyweds. Our first Christmas in our new house and playing Santa for our four little ones. Our first Christmas with Grandma in our home—her first as a widow. Our first Christmas with a baby born that day. There was joy.

But then, full circle, it was our first Christmas alone together.

I sat on the floor that Christmas with a small bundle of treasures of the season in my lap, loath to put them in place. Fingering each piece—the star, the angel, the ass—and considering the symbol and remembering, I noted my mood swing from lonely reluctance at celebrating the day to one of incredible anticipation.

The star. "And, lo, the star, which they saw in the east, went before them, till it came and stood over where the young child was." (Matthew 2:9.)

I held up my star, mastercrafted in sterling silver from the Metropolitan Museum. It was an etched snowflake star that reminded me of the hundreds of New York youth who had presented it to me during their winterfest conference. A star marked the place where He was. A star gave sign that He was near. People could do that too, I mused, like those youth in a wicked world. I had my reminder, my seasonal symbol that was good for all year.

Frankincense. Exotic, aromatic, bright, white burning, and long lasting light. Frankincense is gum resin from certain trees in certain parts of the Holy Land. I opened the rude skin envelope containing our frankincense from our pilgrimage to Jerusalem. I caressed the lumps, gift of the Magi. "And [they] fell down, and worshipped him:

94

and . . . presented unto him gifts; gold, and frankincense, and myrrh." (Matthew 2:11.)

Frankincense, another symbol of life—worship the Lord. don't get too cozy, too casual. Stand steady and let the flame of worship be bright enough and long enough to make a difference to others. Like the poet's comparison of a hero and a saint. The hero goes through the dark streets of life, lighting lamps for people to see by. The saint is himself a light. Ah, yes, be a light. This is a gift to give Him.

Two turtle doves. The doves in my lap were homespun cotton, hand embroidered by Guatemalan native women earning a coin for their keep. Turtle doves for Christmas? Turtle doves for remembrance? "And when the days of her purification . . . were accomplished, they brought him to Jerusalem, to present him to the Lord. . . . and to offer a sacrifice . . . , a pair of turtledoves." (Luke 2:22, 24.)

All of which suggests the mission of Christ.

One Christmas Eve I drove down a small hill near our home in the season's worst snowstorm. Deep drifts made it treacherous at best. Ahead of me at the bus stop stood an elderly neighbor lady. I skidded to a stop, rolled down my window, and, calling her by name, invited her to ride with me. She stoutly refused. I assured her that wherever she was going, I could get her there with good snow tires and front-wheel drive. She was going to the hospital, as was her practice, to rock the new ba-

bies. I coaxed her further to get in the car. At last she confessed, "I can't. I am an eighty-five-year-old woman. If I ride with you today, I'll forget how to take the bus tomorrow. And I have to be at the hospital. Those babies so fresh from heaven need a lot of rocking. No thanks, I'll have to wait for the bus."

There were ways out of loneliness and things to be done that only lonely people had time enough to do. I felt my heart warming toward the season.

The ass. The donkey in my lap was woven in Mexico from straw and boasted the jaunty stance that primitive art lends creatures. Another donkey in another day carried Mary to Bethlehem. Another carried Christ into Jerusalem shortly before the Crucifixion. "Thy king cometh unto thee, meek, and sitting upon an ass." (Matthew 21:5.)

Christmas was the reminding time to bear each other's burdens, meekly and in love. What is given to others is given to Him.

One year's church Christmas pageant came to mind. Frankie was one of the shepherds who insisted upon straightening the aluminum foil crook of his neighbor shepherd, who cried while Frankie laughed. Finally the teacher became openly annoyed at repeatedly bending the foil back into a crook only to have Frankie straighten it out again. She scolded him severely enough to stir up the sympathy of the "little Mary," who put her arm around Frankie and chided the teacher, "You shouldn't get so angry. It's Christmas, you know."

Shepherds. Caring people, shepherds. Like bishops, teachers, and a beautiful young woman down the street shepherding three little ones—alone now, for a time at least. I picked up the worn card hidden in the bundle and read the moving words by some forgotten scribe:

When the song of the angel is stilled
When the star in the sky is gone
When the kings and princes are home
When the shepherds are back with their
    flock
The work of Christmas begins
To find the lost
To heal the broken
To feed the hungry
To release the prisoner
To rebuild the nations
To bring peace among brothers
To make music in the heart.

The angel. I stroked my angel, pitiful now with tarnished tinsel and back scarred where wings had been cut off in a teaching moment. This precious gift from a great friend was brought from Podesta's Christmas shop in San Francisco. I loved this angel, and it reminded me that I had *lived!* The word *angel* comes from the root meaning "messenger" or "instructor." Joseph was instructed by angels about Mary's condition. Angels instructed shepherds about prophecy and the fulfillment of promises, angels singing their good tidings of great joy that first Christmas.

The first Christmas meant joy at each stage of life under each circumstance.

One can't go back, but one can go forward. I would be a shepherd. I would forget myself in bearing the burdens of others. I would be a star, a light, and mark for others the place where He is.

The quaint bundle in my lap seemed to flow of its own light, each piece lending a halo upon the next. Looking at the pieces, remembering the lessons in angels, stars, and beasts of burden, my happiness at that moment measured greater than the sum of the symbols. They are the roots of my joy.

A DEPRESSION ERA CHRISTMAS

Arch L. Madsen

My choicest Christmas memories center around a beautiful brown-eyed girl of eighteen. We've now shared some fifty Christmases. But a very memorable Christmas in my younger days seems appropriate for retelling—the Christmas of 1933. A few words of background explain why.

We were in the depths of the Depression, with economic conditions totally unimaginable today to those who did not actually live through them. Unemployment in Utah that Christmas exceeded 30 percent. This was real unemployment, as it was understood at that critical time that there could be only one breadwinner in a family. Beginning in 1929, the bottom fell out of our country's economic well-being, and it took several years for the terrible impact to hit all of us.

In the spring of 1932 I graduated from high school under most unusual circumstances. Our school district had exhausted all of its money three weeks before our scheduled graduation. State law required a specific number of weeks' instruction to qualify us for graduation. How grateful I am to those caring teachers who continued to work without pay for three weeks so we could officially graduate and receive high school diplomas.

The summer of 1932 was rough. Work for money was almost impossible to find. During that summer I worked in the fields and orchards. Most of the time I was paid in kind: hay, apples, peaches, etc., which was most welcome in our family of eight children. How my mother ever prepared over nine hundred meals a month and how she kept us alive I'll never know! My father, a salesman, was bringing home about fifty dollars a month.

During that summer of working from daylight to dark, I was able to earn in cash about fourteen dollars. I wanted very much to go to Brigham Young University, but as the summer passed, hopes dimmed. Still, I believed part-time employment at BYU or arrangements for a student loan would develop. Five minutes in the office of the person in charge of such hopes quickly dashed them all.

Completely discouraged, I walked slowly from the Maeser Building on

97

"Temple Hill" (the name for the area where the BYU campus is now located). I stopped at the home of my dearest friend who had introduced me to the world of amateur radio. His mother asked what classes I had registered for, and when I told her none because I had no money, she said, "Oh, yes you do!" and wrote me a check for thirty-two dollars to cover a quarter's tuition. My fourteen dollars was adequate for me to participate in what we called "Book Clubs"—for each class, five of us would purchase one text and rotate it.

At the end of the winter quarter in March 1933, all the money had disappeared and things looked very bleak. But thanks to my friend, there was a silver lining. Through him I became a civilian attached to the U.S. Army Signal Corps, as a part of the CCC (Civilian Conservation Corps). Our pay would be twenty-five dollars a month, food, and a place to sleep. Twenty dollars of my money would be sent home to help the family, and I could keep five dollars. When I learned of this opportunity, I was so excited I couldn't sleep the first night.

My friend and I were sent to Fort Missoula, Montana, to build from his personal resources their first military point-to-point radio communications station and to open this station.

As Christmas of 1933 approached, I learned that special railroad fares were available for the holidays! What a thrill this brought! The day before Christmas I arrived at the Union Pacific depot to be greeted by three members of my family in the old family car. I was surprised it had made it to Salt Lake City. How well I remember that morning! When I stepped out of the station, the black smoke cloud hanging over the city was so dense I couldn't see the towers of the temple from two blocks away. At that time, practically all homes were heated by burning coal.

With the luxury of a few dollars in my pocket, Christmas coming, and a wonderful family of parents and seven younger brothers and sisters, what should I do? In my younger life I had long envied those who had received an electric train for Christmas, and I knew my own brothers and sisters would enjoy such a gift.

After spending most of the day shopping in all the stores, I found a tiny train with a transformer and a few feet of circular track at a price I could afford—$4.95.

Time and special blessings have dramatically changed that economic situation. But the Christmas of 1933 will ever remain a day of joy as I remember watching my happy brothers and sisters playing with a *real* electric train.

THE REAL CHRISTMAS OF 1933

Elder Richard Lindsay

The year 1933 had been a difficult one for our family. The previous winter my father had died suddenly, leaving my widowed mother with six young children, ranging in age from four to fourteen. Ten days after my father's death, my oldest brother, fourteen, who was to be the new "head of the house," died unexpectedly from an acute illness.

The Depression, with all its devastating consequences to happy family life, continued to exact its toll of discouragement, frustration and demoralization. Many of our neighbors, in the absence of employment, or with lifetime savings lost in failed banks, were unable to meet payments on their homes or unable to pay their taxes. My mother was struggling to save our home, where she and my father had moved immediately after their marriage and where the beginnings of a satisfying and blessed family life had begun.

Prior to marriage my mother had trained in Michigan to become a registered nurse. This was considered an unusual accomplishment for a Utah girl, especially when professional training was not offered in the state.

Unable in this Depression year to find regular employment to support her large family, my mother would accept jobs to do "home nursing" for families experiencing serious illnesses yet who were unable to afford regular hospital care. With a combination of fatigue from such efforts, plus the responsibility of caring for her own family, Mother's own health was at the breaking point.

As a child, I wondered what else could happen to make life more difficult. In this otherwise discouraging setting, I remember seeing a relief truck parked in front of the elementary school across the street. It was loaded with fresh-dressed turkeys that were to be distributed to needy families—those whose family heads were out of work.

I reported this happy development to my mother, who was ill and in bed. I felt that I had scouted out the answer to our Christmas feast, which would help alleviate the depressing circumstances in which our family had been placed.

My mother used the moment to impart a great principle which I have tried to retain throughout my life. "Richard," she said, "we are not a poor family we are just a family that has experienced some temporary misfortune. Those turkeys are for the people who *really* need them. We have a fine red rooster in the chicken coop, and you and your brother can help prepare him for a real Christmas dinner."

By present standards our family Christmas that year would be considered somber. The few Christmas gifts largely included clothing necessities and fresh fruit. The important ingredients for a great Christmas celebration were still in place, however. Our home was warm, and we had coal in the basement to last the winter. Mother's health was improving, and we had been able to pay the taxes on our home. In addition, I had saved a whole dollar from work projects I had been able to locate, and with that purchased thirteen presents for family members, including a twenty-five-cent bottle of "Italian Balm" for my mother.

On Christmas my mother expressed a prayer of thanks for the rich blessings our family had received, and prayed for those who were truly needy. In subsequent years when the material blessings of life have been more abundant, I have still reflected on the "Real Christmas of 1933."

THE ANGEL TREE

Ariel Bybee

Neylan was almost five when I first took her to see the Angel Tree at the Metropolitan Museum of Art.

We had lived in New York City for almost seven years, and even though I had heard that the Angel Tree was a must for viewing at Christmastime, I had never been to see it, even by myself. But this Christmas holiday, my husband was out of town for a few days on a business trip, our daughter Neylan was on vacation, and she and I had a free afternoon.

We slipped into a cab from our Westside apartment and were across the park in no time. Luckily, the museum was not crowded. Saturdays, Sundays, and holidays are a madhouse at the Met, but this afternoon (it must have been a Tuesday or Wednesday) there was no line at the ticket booth. We dutifully pinned on our buttons showing that we had paid the suggested donation, and I asked the security guard directions to the Angel Tree. He nodded his head straight back several times and rolled his eyes up, leaving me with the distinct impression that he had been making the same gesture all afternoon.

We were excited with anticipation as we briskly walked hand-in-hand in the direction the guard had indicated. In no time we saw a sign with an arrow pointing to the "Medieval Hall." We heard faint music in the background. As we stood in the arched entryway of the hall, we had our first glimpse of the Angel Tree. It was magical! A feeling of reverence enveloped us as we stood trying to take in the calm and beauty of the scene.

The large, radiant Christmas tree directly in front of us was ideally placed as the centerpiece of a vast medieval-style hall. The hall is patterned after the fifteenth-century cathedrals of Spain. It had been built as part of the museum in 1956 to display a choir screen that had been brought from the Cathedral of Valladolid in Spain. This massive wrought-iron screen divides the hall in two and provides a perfect backdrop for the brilliantly lit tree decked with eighteenth-century Neapolitan figures.

The tree sits on an elegantly carved wooden base. Statues of biblical figures adorn the walls and pillars of the hall. Other than the artificial candles on the tree, the only illumination in the room itself comes from stylistic skylights that permit rays of sunlight to jet down onto the many gracefully carved sculptures. Clouds change the light, moment by moment, focusing it on a figure here, then there, as though a tour guide were directing our view. We heard an organ playing Christmas carols. Baroque sounds were echoing through the walls as though we were hearing one of the organs in the cavernous cathedrals of Europe. It was into this solemn setting that we, mother and daughter, stepped.

Without thinking, still hand-in-hand, we made our way to the base of the giant blue spruce so that we could see up close the faces of exquisitely sculpted terra cotta angels and colorful lifelike figures enacting the wondrous events of the birth of the Savior.

We examined each of the nativity figures, the tallest being no more than twenty inches. They number almost two hundred and form the landscape upon which the Angel Tree sits. Each handcrafted figure is a treasured work of art. The angels with their delicately draped robes and flexible bodies sit gracefully on the tree boughs. They gesture in expectation and adoration toward the Baby Jesus in his manger.

With childlike enthusiasm, my little one would whisper, "Mommy, look over here at these little sheep." And I would whisper back, "Oh, come over here and see this group of wise men."

The faces of the people in this Neapolitan landscape we observed seemed to be realistic, but the angels seemed to

have been crafted with celestial expressions. They had parted lips, rounded cheeks, eyes filled with wonder — expressions of joy and amazement.

After we had surveyed every gem on and around the treasured tree right up to the glittering star at the top, I assumed my little one would be weary and ready for the ride home. But, at the suggestion of leaving, she turned to another part of the hall, pointed up to one of the large fifteenth-century sculptures, and asked, "Isn't that Mary and Baby Jesus?" There were six structural pillars evenly spaced throughout the hall.

This particular sculpture to which she was referring was resting on a pedestal just in front of one of these pillars. It was a "Virgin and Child" of exquisite beauty! I lifted my forty-three-pounder into my arms so that she could see, eye-to-eye, Mary holding her infant son. With no sign of fatigue and with the same contagious enthusiasm she had viewed the Angel Tree, she quizzed me about this inspired work of art. I read from the card at the base that it had been carved in France from 1415 to 1417. "It was made of limestone," I read, "and was polychromed and gilded." I explained, as she listened with rapt attention, that "polychromed" meant the statue had originally been painted with many colors and that it had at one time had some gold leaf on it. She pointed out to me some traces of polychroming still noticeable in the creases of Mary's robe.

I remember as she sat cradled in my arms (much the same way as the limestone Baby Jesus was cradled in his mother's arms) that she sighed, "It's old, but it's still pretty." I agreed.

There were many other "Virgin and Child" sculptures artfully displayed around the pillars in the hall. There must have been eight or ten of them, each a work of great beauty. I decided to play an observation game by asking Neylan if she could tell me which of the statues was made of limestone and which of wood. Had they been polychromed? Were they all French or were some Spanish? How were they the same and how were they different? Which was most beautiful, the favorite? I cheated by reading the answers at the base of each work of art. Together we learned some basics of fifteenth-century French and Spanish sculpture.

My arms were getting shaky, and her concentration was waning as we glanced back at the heavenly scene that had brought us to the Medieval Hall. We walked out of the museum filled with the spirit of Christmas and the fulfillment of sharing a joyful experience together.

Now, several years later, it seems strange to me that Neylan barely remembers that December afternoon at all! It is so vivid in my mind because I was seeing it through her eyes as well as my own. I experienced my child's joy with a knowledge that she could not. I also experienced the joy of seeing it for the first time. For me, that made each detail of our visit doubly intense.

One thing is for sure, however: the first thing the little girl who is now a teenager wants to do every Christmas season is to visit the Angel Tree at the Metropolitan Museum of Art.

IN THE SPIRIT OF CHRISTMAS

Hannelore Janke

This was not the time to be sad. Next month I'd be turning twelve; it was time to give up dolls anyway. As I carefully folded the doll clothes I had sewn for Lilo, I realized that we had hardly played together these past six months; maybe we wouldn't miss each other too much, especially since she was going to get a new mom for Christmas.

Lieselotte, Lilo for short, was neither the prettiest nor the biggest of my dolls. She didn't even have real hair. But Lilo was the only doll that had survived the war with me. In fact, it was her size, about ten inches, and her plainness that had saved her life.

When the approaching Russian troops had forced us to flee our home in West Prussia, in January of this year, 1945, we could take only a few belongings, such as a change of clothing—whatever would fit into our knapsacks. It still surprises me that Mom let me stuff Lilo into the little space I had left on top of my pack. It also still surprises me that Lilo didn't get lost in the commotion of overfilled trains and crowded refugee camps. Many children became separated from their families in those

days, but Lilo and I arrived together in the small town in central Germany that was to become our new home.

We stayed in this last refugee camp only four days, and then all five of us—Mom, my two younger brothers, and Lilo and I—were given a room in a spacious, old house with a family that had a son my age, Joachim. His cousins from Berlin, Dieter and Hans, who had lost their home to air raids, were also living there, and the four of us became the best of friends.

Having boys as buddies was a new experience for me. Where I had played mostly with dolls before, I now played cops and robbers. We occupied our time with cards and board games, always looking for a new hideout somewhere in the lush yard or the spacious attic. Joachim's train set and his lead soldiers also got a frequent workout. As a lawyer's son, Joachim had a substantial collection of books, and the boys enticed me to read about cowboys and Indians and got me hooked on adventure stories. Was it any wonder that Lilo spent most of the summer by herself?

And it was an endless summer. Because of the chaos after Germany's unconditional surrender in the spring of 1945, our summer vacation lasted from April until October.

It wasn't all fun and games, though. Scouting for food was the main occupation for Mom and me during harvest time. The food we were able to buy with our ration cards was barely enough for one meal a day. In order to survive, we had to spend most of our time in the fields and forests that surrounded our new hometown. We gathered mushrooms and picked berries and rose hips; we helped a nearby farmer harvest potatoes and sugar beets in exchange for food; we gleaned wheat by hand and took the wheat berries to the ancient windmill up on the hill to trade for flour. We made jam from the rose hips and molasses from the sugar beets, and put the mushrooms on strings to hang up for drying.

But no matter how hard we worked to survive and to prepare for the long winter ahead, what we were able to stash away lasted only a few months. Dad, who had been drafted to serve in the German Army, got captured at the end of the war and was still in prison camp. He couldn't help provide for us, and my two brothers were only four and six years old. So by the time Christmas rolled around, we were hungry again. That's when I decided to trade Lilo for food.

I was too young to know my way around the Black Market; however, during the four days we had spent in the refugee camp, we had met a woman who I felt would be able to help me. As a single mother with two small children, she had learned some survival shortcuts, and because she needed a Christmas present for her little girl, she was delighted to make a deal with me. I expected her this afternoon, as soon as she was able to get some food from the Black Market. Lilo was packed and ready to go.

What a sad and happy day. I had to say good-bye to Lilo, and I received two loaves of bread. It was a good deal, because on the Black Market a loaf of bread cost thirty times more than on ration cards.

Now I could make plans for Christmas. One loaf was for Mom and the boys. Because I was in the middle of a growing spurt and would get so hungry that my knees became weak and shaky, Mom wanted me to keep the other loaf. How rich I felt having my own food to eat and to share! Of course, I wanted to share it also with my buddies. It was the only Christmas present I had for them.

I proudly cut three slices of my heavy, whole-grain bread. Wrapping paper was not available in any form, so I placed the slices on a plate I had decorated with small pine boughs. Mom gave me a little of our last rose-hip jam. I put a dab of it on each piece. Now I was ready for Christmas Eve, which is the high point of a German Christmas.

I was so happy to have a surprise for my friends. I had no idea that they would also have a surprise for me. I had not expected any presents; having come through the war alive was the greatest gift.

But on Christmas Eve I received a tray decorated with small pine boughs and loaded with treasures. Of all the Christmas gifts I have received since then, in over forty years, the simple presents on that tray moved me the most: a pencil stub, a sheet of used carbon paper, half a scratch pad, and a book from Joachim's library. The memory of that Christmas Eve still fills me with the joy that comes from caring and sharing. Each one of us shared our last precious possessions. Because of that, the Christmas of 1945 is the one I remember best.